International acclaim for Mourid Barghouti's

I SAW RAMALLAH

"Stirring. . . . Poignant. . . . Compelling. . . . *I Saw Ramallah* is a magnificent addition to world literature. It is picturesque and lifelike. Its evocative images touch, move, and inspire."
—*Middle East Studies Association Bulletin*

"Marvelous. . . . A beautifully constructed and moving memoir."
—*Al-Ahram Weekly*

"An honest and lyrical account from the Palestinian Diaspora. . . . This book describes in detail the damage done to the Palestinian people in the most beautiful prose. . . . Because of his frankness and calm tone, Barghouti has ensured that this life story will stay with the reader a long time after all the shouting and politicking stops." —*Cairo Times*

"A rare memoir. . . . Humane and eloquent." —*In These Times*

"Barghouti's account is controlled, reflective, factual, unemotional, eloquent. . . . It has been superbly and sensitively translated." —*The Times Literary Supplement*

Mourid Barghouti

I SAW RAMALLAH

TRANSLATED FROM THE ARABIC BY AHDAF SOUEIF
WITH A FOREWORD BY EDWARD W. SAID

Mourid Barghouti was born in the West Bank in 1944 and graduated from Cairo University in 1967. His poems have been published in Beirut, Amman, and Cairo, and his collected works were published in Beirut in 1997. He lives in Cairo.

Ahdaf Soueif was born in Cairo and educated in Egypt and England. She is the author of the novels *In the Eye of the Sun* and *The Map of Love* and the story collections *Aisha* and *Sandpiper.*

Edward W. Said is University Professor of English and Comparative Literature at Columbia University. He is the author of more than twenty books, including *Orientalism, Culture and Imperialism,* and a memoir, *Out of Place.*

I SAW RAMALLAH

I SAW RAMALLAH

Mourid Barghouti

TRANSLATED BY
Ahdaf Soueif

WITH A FOREWORD BY
Edward W. Said

ANCHOR BOOKS

A Division of Random House, Inc.

New York

FIRST ANCHOR BOOKS EDITION, MAY 2003

Library of Congress Cataloging-in-Publication Data
Barghuthi, Murid.
[Ra'aytu Ram Allah. English]
I saw Ramallah / Mourid Barghouti ; translated by Ahdaf Soueif ;
with a foreword by Edward W. Said.
p. cm.
ISBN 1-4000-3266-0
1. Barghâthâ, Murâd—Journeys—West Bank.
2. West Bank—Description and travel.
3. Barghâthâ, Murâd—Political and social views.
I. Soueif, Ahdaf. II. Title.
PJ7816.A682 R3313 2003
892.7'8603—dc21
2002034226
CIP

www.anchorbooks.com

Printed in the United States of America
10 9 8 7 6 5 4 3 2 1

CONTENTS

FOREWORD

Edward W. Said

This compact, intensely lyrical narrative of a return from pro-
tracted exile abroad to Ramallah on the West Bank in the
summer of 1996 is one of the finest existential accounts of
Palestinian displacement that we now have. It is by Mourid
Barghouti, a well-known poet who, as he says here and there in the
book, is married to Radwa Ashour, the distinguished Egyptian academic and novelist; the two were students of English literature
together at Cairo University in the 1960s, and for a period of seventeen years during their marriage lived apart from each other, he as
PLO representative in Budapest, she and their son Tamim in Cairo,
where she is professor of English at Ain Shams University. The
political reasons for the separation are alluded to in *I Saw Ramallah*,
as are the circumstances of his exile from the West Bank as well, of
course, as his return thirty years later. Widely and enthusiastically
received all over the Arab world when it appeared in 1997, the book
went on to win the Naguib Mahfouz Medal for Literature, one of the
most satisfying parts of which is this elegant and compelling English

translation by Ahdaf Soueif, herself an important Egyptian novelist and critic whose own work (notably *In the Eye of the Sun* and *The Map of Love*) is in English. It is therefore an important literary event to have these two talents contained within the same cover. I am delighted to be able to say a few prefatory words about this work.

Having myself made a similar trip to Jerusalem (after an absence of forty-five years), I very well know the admixture of emotions—happiness, of course, regret, sorrow, surprise, anger, among others—that accompanies such a return. The great novelty and power of Barghouti's book is that it painstakingly chronicles, and gives clarity to, the whirlwind of sensations and thoughts that otherwise overwhelm one on such occasions. Palestine after all is no ordinary place. It is steeped in all the known histories and traditions of monotheism, and has seen conquerors and civilizations of every stripe come and go. In the twentieth century it has been the site of an unremitting contest between the indigenous Arab inhabitants, who were tragically dispossessed and mostly dispersed in 1948, and an incoming political movement of Zionist Jews, of largely European provenance, who set up a Jewish state there and, in 1967, conquered the West Bank and Gaza, which they in effect still hold. Every Palestinian today is therefore in the unusual position of knowing that there was once a Palestine and yet seeing that place with a new name, people, and identity that deny Palestine altogether. A 'return' to Palestine is therefore an unusual, not to say urgently fraught, occurrence.

Barghouti's narrative in a sense was made possible because of the grotesquely misnamed 'peace process' between Yasser 'Arafat's PLO and the state of Israel. Begun in September 1993 and continuing unresolved as I write (in early August 2000), this US-brokered arrangement neither provided for real Palestinian sovereignty in

Gaza and the West Bank nor allowed for peace and reconciliation between Jews and Arabs. But it did allow for the return of some Palestinians from the 1967 territories to their homes, and it is this happy fact that triggers the border scenes with which *I Saw Ramallah* opens. As Barghouti quickly discovers, the irony is that even though there are Palestinian officers at the Jordan River bridge separating the Hashemite Kingdom from Palestine, Israeli military men and women are still in charge. As he tersely notes, "the others are still masters of the place." Yet whereas he is a West Banker and can make the visit he so eloquently narrates here, the overwhelming majority of most Palestinians (about 3.5 million) are refugees from the 1948 territories and therefore cannot return under the present circumstances.

Necessarily, there is a good deal of politics in Barghouti's book, but none of it is either abstract or ideologically driven: whatever comes up about politics arises from the lived circumstances of Palestinian life, which, most often, is surrounded by restrictions having to do with travel and residence. Both of these related matters, taken for granted by most people in the world who are citizens, have passports, and can travel freely without thinking about who they are all the time, are extraordinarily charged for the stateless Palestinians, many of whom do in fact have passports but nevertheless, like the millions of refugees all over the Arab world, Europe, Australia, North and South America, still bear the onus of being displaced and hence, misplaced. Barghouti's text is consequently laced with problems related to where he can or cannot stay, where he may or may not go, for how long and in what circumstances he must leave, and what, most of all, occurs when he is not there. His brother Mounif dies an unnecessary and cruel death in France because no one can (or will) get to him and help.

Major figures of cultural importance like the assassinated novelist Ghassan Kanafani and the cartoonist Naji al-'Ali haunt the book as well, reminders that no matter how gifted and artistically endowed Palestinians are, they are still subject to sudden death and unexplained disappearance. Hence also the intermittently grieving, sorrowful tone of this book, otherwise so exuberant and celebratory.

Yet what gives this book an unmistakable stamp of profound authenticity is its life-affirming poetic texture. Barghouti's writing is really amazingly free of bitterness or recrimination; he neither reproves and harangues Israelis for what they have done nor berates the Palestinian leadership for the bizarre arrangements they agreed to on the ground. He is of course absolutely correct to note several times that settlements dot (and usually disfigure) the gently rolling and often mountainous Palestinian landscape, but that is all he does, in addition to noting what is an inconvenient fact for the supposed peacemakers to deal with, especially since places like Ramallah and Deir Ghassanah are so indomitably, unchangingly Palestinian. There is no small irony in play when he excavates the etymology of his family name. (Although I have no firm information about this, I think the Barghoutis constitute the single largest Palestinian family, with estimated numbers running as high as 25,000.) He cannot get away from the fact that it seems to derive from the Arabic word for 'flea,' and this humbling detail strangely gives the narrative even more humanity and poignancy.

For it is as·an account of loss in the midst of return and reunion that *I Saw Ramallah* gets its main distinction. And it is Barghouti's extended rebuttal and resistance against the reasons for that loss that endows his poetry with substance and gives this narrative its positive valence. "The Occupation," he says, "has created generations of us that have to adore an unknown beloved: distant, difficult, surrounded by guards, by walls, by nuclear missiles, by sheer terror." Therefore, in his poems and in this prose accompaniment to his return he seeks to break down the walls, evade the guards, gain access to *his* Palestine, which he finds in Ramallah. Once a quiet garden suburb of Jerusalem, Ramallah has in recent years become the center of Palestinian urban life. It has relative autonomy, a decent amount of cultural activity, and a rapidly increasing population. So it is in this newly invigorated and rediscovered Ramallah that Barghouti the exile and dispossessed writer finds himself anew—only to find himself again and again in the new forms of his displacement. "It is enough for a person to go through the first experience of uprooting, to become uprooted forever." Thus despite its joy and moments of exuberance this narrative return at bottom reenacts exile rather than repatriation. This is what gives it both its tragic dimension and its appealing precariousness. Ahdaf Soueif's excellent translation makes precisely this rather special tone available now to readers of English. The Palestinian experience is therefore humanized and given substance in a new way.

New York, August 11, 2000

I Saw Ramallah

THE BRIDGE

It is very hot on the bridge. A drop of sweat slides from my forehead down to the frame of my spectacles, then the lens. A mist envelops what I see, what I expect, what I remember. The view here shimmers with scenes that span a lifetime; a lifetime spent trying to get here. Here I am, crossing the Jordan River. I hear the creak of the wood under my feet. On my left shoulder a small bag. I walk westward in a normal manner—or rather, a manner that appears normal. Behind me the world, ahead of me my world.

The last thing I remember of this bridge is that I crossed it on my way from Ramallah to Amman thirty years ago. From Amman I went to Cairo and back to college. I was in my fourth and final year at Cairo University.

The morning of June 5, 1967: the Latin exam. Only a few left to go: Latin, then two days later 'the Novel,' then 'Drama.' And then I would have kept my promise to Mounif and fulfilled my mother's wish to see one of her sons a college graduate. The previous exams— History of European Civilization, Poetry, Literary Criticism, and

Translation—had gone by with no surprises. Nearly there. After the results come out I shall go back to Amman, and from there—across this same bridge—to Ramallah, where I learn from my parents' letters that they have started to decorate our apartment in al-Liftawi's building in preparation for my return with the Certificate.

It is very hot in the examination hall. A drop of sweat slides down my brow to the frame of my spectacles. It stops, then slides down the lens, and from there to the Latin words in the exam paper: altus, alta, altum—but what is this noise outside? Explosions? Are these the maneuvers of the Egyptian Army? The talk in the last few days has all been of war. Is it war? I wipe my spectacles with a tissue, check through my answers, and leave my seat. I hand my paper to the monitor. A flake of yellow paint from the ceiling falls onto the exam papers on the table between us. He looks up at the ceiling in disgust and I walk out.

I walk down the steps of the Faculty of Arts. Madame Aisha—our middle-aged colleague who enrolled in the university after her husband's death—is sitting in her car under the campus palm trees. She calls out to me in her French accent and disturbed manner: "Mourid! Mourid! War has broken out. We've brought down twenty-three planes!"

I lean into the car, holding onto the door. Ahmad Sa'id is ecstatic on the car radio. The patriotic anthems ring loud. A group of students collect around us. Comments fly around, assured and doubtful. I tighten my right fist on the bottle of Pelican ink that is always with me in the exams. Until this day I do not know why with my arm I drew a wide arc in the air and, aiming at the trunk of that palm tree, hurled the bottle of ink with all my strength so in that midnight-blue collision it burst into fragments of glass that settled on the lawn.

And from here, from Voice of the Arabs radio station, Ahmad Sa'id tells me that Ramallah is no longer mine and that I will not return to it. The city has fallen.

The examinations are suspended for weeks. The examinations resume. I graduate. I am awarded a BA from the Department of English Language and Literature, and I fail to find a wall on which to hang my certificate.

Those who happened to be outside the homeland when war broke out try in every possible way to get a reunion permit. They try through their relatives in Palestine and through the Red Cross. Some—like my brother Majid—dare to take the risk of smuggling themselves in.

Israel allows in hundreds of elderly people and forbids hundreds of thousands of young people to return. And the world finds a name for us. They called us *naziheen*, the displaced ones.

Displacement is like death. One thinks it happens only to other people. From the summer of '67 I became that displaced stranger whom I had always thought was someone else.

The stranger is the person who renews his Residence Permit. He fills out forms and buys the stamps for them. He has to constantly come up with evidence and proofs. He is the one who is always asked: "And where are you from, brother?" Or he is asked: "Are summers hot in your country?" He does not care for the details that concern the people of the country where he finds himself or for their 'domestic' policy. But he is the first to feel its consequences. He may not rejoice in what makes them happy but he is always afraid when they are afraid. He is always the 'infiltrating element' in demonstrations, even if he never left his house that day. He is the one whose relationship with places is distorted, he gets attached to them and repulsed by them at the same time. He is the one who cannot tell his story in a continuous narrative and lives hours in every moment. Every moment for him has its passing immortality. His memory resists ordering. He lives essentially in that hidden, silent spot within himself. He is careful of his mystery and dislikes those who probe into it. He lives the details of another life that does not interest those around him, and when he speaks he screens those details rather than declare them. He loves the ringing of the telephone, yet fears it. The stranger is told by kind people: "You are in your second home here and among your kin." He is despised for being a stranger, or sympathized with for being a stranger. The second is harder to bear than the first.

At noon on that Monday I was struck by displacement.

Was I mature enough to realize that there were strangers like me living in their own capitals? Their countries unoccupied by foreign forces? Did Abu Hayyan al-Tawhidi look into the future and write—in his distant past—our current estrangement in the second half of the twentieth century? Is this second half longer than the first? I do not know.

But I do know that the stranger can never go back to what he was. Even if he returns. It is over. A person gets 'displacement' as he gets asthma, and there is no cure for either. And a poet is worse off, because poetry itself is an estrangement. Where does asthma come into it? Is it the coughing fit I had while waiting those long hours on the Jordanian bank before the 'other side' (as they are called by the Palestinian police) would permit my feet to touch this boundary between two times?

I had arrived from Amman to this Jordanian side of the bridge. My brother 'Alaa drove me. His wife, Elham, and my mother were with us. We left our house in Shmaysani at nine-fifteen in the morn-

4

ing and got here before ten. This was the farthest point they were allowed to reach. I said goodbye, and they turned back to Amman.

I sat in a waiting-room set up exactly at the end of the bridge. I asked the Jordanian officer about the next step.

"You wait here till we receive a signal from them, then you cross the bridge."

I waited a while in the room before I realized it was going to be a long wait. I went to the door and stood looking at the river.

I was not surprised by its narrowness: the Jordan was always a very thin river. This is how we knew it in childhood. The surprise was that after these long years it had become a river without water. Almost without water. Nature had colluded with Israel in stealing its water. It used to have a voice, now it was a silent river, a river like a parked car.

The other bank displays itself clearly to the eye. And the eye sees what it sees. Friends who had crossed the river after a long absence told me they had wept here.

I did not weep.

That slight numbness did not rise from my chest to my eyes. No one was with me to tell me what my face looked like during those hours of waiting.

I look at the body of the bridge. Will I really cross it? Will there be some last-minute problem? Will they send me back? Will they invent a procedural error? Shall I actually walk on that other bank, on those hills displaying themselves in front of me?

There is no topological difference between this Jordanian land I stand on and that Palestinian land on the other side of the bridge.

That, then, is the 'Occupied Territory.'

Toward the end of 1979 I was at a conference of the Union of Arab Writers in Damascus. Our hosts took us to visit the city of

Qunaytera. A convoy of cars took us on the short journey and we saw the destruction visited by the Israelis on the city. We stood by the barbed wire behind which flew the Israeli flag. I stretched my hand across the wire and took hold of a shrub growing wild on the occupied side of the Golan. I shook the shrub and said to Hussein Muruwwa, who stood next to me: "Here is the Occupied Territory, Abu Nizar; I can hold it with my hand!"

When you hear on the radio and read in newspapers and magazines and books and speeches the words 'the Occupied Territories' year after year, and festival after festival, and summit conference after summit conference, you think it's somewhere at the end of the earth. You think there is absolutely no way you can get to it. Do you see how close it is? How touchable? How real? I can hold it in my hand, like a handkerchief.

In the eyes of Hussein Muruwwa the answer formed itself, and it was silent and moist.

Now here I am looking at it: at the west bank of the Jordan River. This then is the 'Occupied Territory'? No one was with me to whom I could repeat what I had said years ago to Hussein Muruwwa: that it was not just a phrase on the news bulletins. When the eye sees it, it has all the clarity of earth and pebbles and hills and rocks. It has its colors and its temperatures and its wild plants too.

Who would dare make it into an abstraction now that it has declared its physical self to the senses?

It is no longer 'the beloved' in the poetry of resistance, or an item on a political party program, it is not an argument or a metaphor. It stretches before me, as touchable as a scorpion, a bird, a well; visible as a field of chalk, as the prints of shoes.

I asked myself, what is so special about it except that we have lost it?

It is a land, like any land.

We sing for it only so that we may remember the humiliation of having had it taken from us. Our song is not for some sacred thing of the past but for our current self-respect that is violated anew every day by the Occupation.

Here it is in front of me, as it has been since the day of creation. I said to myself: "Land does not move away." I have not reached it yet. I merely see it directly. I am like someone who has been told he has won a large prize, only he has not got it in his hands yet.

I am still on the Jordanian side. The hours pass. I go back to the waiting room. It is clear there is nothing new for me. I sit on the chair and take out my papers. I pass the time in leafing through them: epigrams and poetic 'sketches' I am preparing for publication under the title "The Logic of Beings"—my ninth volume of poetry. I cast a quick look over the lines and return the papers to the bag. The anxiety of waiting reflects into an anxiety about the work. Before publication I lose my enthusiasm and doubt the value of the text that is about to escape from my control.

I love the poem as it forms under my fingers, image after image, word after word. And then fear arrives and certainty disappears. That contented moment when the creator is fascinated by his creation ends for me.

This happens and has happened since the first poem I ever published. I remember it well.

I was in the fourth and final year at university. I used to read some of my poems to Radwa on the steps of the library and she used to assure me they were good poems and that I would definitely—one day—be a poet. And one day I gave one of my poems to Farouk 'Abd al-Wahab to publish in *Theater Magazine*, which was edited by Rashad Rushdi. And then I spent days of terror.

Every day I would think of asking for the poem back, but I was afraid he would consider me weak and indecisive. I would see him in college and almost ask what he thought of the poem and stop myself at the last moment. From the second that poem left my hands I felt it was no good and should not be published. Now I know it really was bad.

The days passed until we arrived at Monday, June 5, 1967.

I went to a baker to stock up with bread, for we thought we were in for a long war. I stood in the long queue and on the pavement beside me—an extension of a small bookshop that had stayed open—were piles of newspapers, magazines, and books. Among tens of magazines I saw the *Theater Magazine*. I paid for it and riffled through the pages looking for my poem and—I found it. "Mourid al-Barghouti: 'Apology to a Faraway Soldier.'" What coincidence is this?

My first poem published on this strange morning. On the cover of the magazine, the date: Monday, June 5, 1967. A journalist once asked me about this. I told him the story, then added, joking: "I wonder if the Arabs were defeated and Palestine was lost because I wrote a poem."

We laughed, and did not laugh.

I leave the room again.

I go for a walk in the small space between the room and the river. I contemplate the scene. I have nothing to do except contemplate.

A desert land so close to the water. And the sun a scorpion.

"*Tell the eye of the sun . . .* "—that sad song which became an elegy for men lost in another desert not so far from this place comes to my mind. June 19, 1967: a knock on the door of my flat in Zamalek brings in a man of strange aspect and clothing, his face burned by the sun. I embrace him as though he had descended

8

directly from a cloud and into my arms: "How did you get here, *Khali* 'Ata?"

He had walked for fourteen days in the desert of Sinai. Since June 5 he had been walking.

"We didn't fight. They destroyed our weapons and chased us with their planes from the first hour . . . ."

My uncle was an officer in the Jordanian army, then—at the beginning of the sixties—went to work as a trainer in the Kuwaiti army. In the '67 war they sent him with the Kuwaiti battalion to fight with Egypt. He said they were now in a camp near Dahshur under the command of the Egyptian Army and did not know what the next step would be.

I did not see any of the returning soldiers except him, and that was enough to sadden the heart. One man was enough to embody the whole idea. The idea of defeat.

It is noon. My tension increases with each new minute of waiting. Will they allow me to cross the river? Why are they so late?

At this point I hear someone call my name: "Take your bag and cross the water."

At last! Here I am, walking, with my small bag, across the bridge. A bridge no longer than a few meters of wood and thirty years of exile.

How was this piece of dark wood able to distance a whole nation from its dreams? To prevent entire generations from taking their coffee in homes that were theirs? How did it deliver us to all this patience and all that death? How was it able to scatter us among exiles, and tents, and political parties, and frightened whispers?

I do not thank you, you short, unimportant bridge. You are not a sea or an ocean that we might find our excuses in your terrors. You are not a mountain range inhabited by wild beasts and fantastical monsters that we might summon our instincts to protect us from you. I would have thanked you, bridge, if you had been on another planet, at a spot the old Mercedes could not reach in thirty minutes. I would have thanked you had you been made by volcanoes and their thick, orange terror. But you were made by miserable carpenters, who held their nails in the corners of their mouths, and their cigarettes behind their ears. I do not say thank you, little bridge. Should I be ashamed in front of you? Or should you be ashamed in front of me? You are near like the stars of the naive poet, far like the step of one paralyzed. What embarrassment is this? I do not forgive you, and you do not forgive me. The sound of the wood under my feet.

Fayruz calls it the Bridge of Return. The Jordanians call it the King Hussein Bridge. The Palestinian Authority calls it al-Karama Crossing. The common people and the bus and taxi drivers call it the Allenby Bridge. My mother, and before her my grandmother and my father and my uncle's wife, Umm Talal, call it simply: the Bridge.

Now I cross it for the first time since thirty summers. The summer of 1966, and immediately after, no slowing down, the summer of 1996.

Here, on these prohibited wooden planks, I walk and chatter my whole life to myself. I chatter my life, without a sound, and without a pause. Moving images appear and disappear without coherence, scenes from an untidy life, a memory that bangs backward and forward like a shuttle. Images shape themselves and resist the editing that would give them final form. Their form is their chaos.

A distant childhood. The faces of friends and enemies. I am the person coming from the continents of others, from their languages and their borders. The person with spectacles on his eyes and a small bag on his shoulder. And these are the planks of the bridge. These are my steps on them. Here I am walking toward the land of the poem. A visitor? A refugee? A citizen? A guest? I do not know.

Is this a political moment? Or an emotional one? Or social? A practical moment? A surreal one? A moment of the body? Or of the mind? The wood creaks. What has passed of life is shrouded in a mist that both hides and reveals. Why do I wish I could get rid of this bag? There is very little water under the bridge. Water without water. As though the water apologized for its presence on this boundary between two histories, two faiths, two tragedies. The scene is of rock. Chalk. Military. Desert. Painful as a toothache.

The Jordanian flag is here: red, white, black, and green; the colors of the Arab Revolt. After a few meters, there is the Israeli flag in the blue of the Nile and the Euphrates with the Star of David between them. One gust of wind moves both flags. *White our deeds, black our battles, green our lands* . . . poetry on the mind. But the scene is as prosaic as a bill of reckoning.

The wooden planks creak beneath my feet.

The June air today boils like the June air yesterday. "*O wooden bridge* . . . ." Suddenly Fayruz is there. Unusually for her, the lyrics of the song are more direct than one would wish. How have they settled in the hearts of intellectuals and peasants and students and soldiers and aunts and revolutionaries? Is it people's need to have their voice heard through listening to it from the mouth of another? Is it their attachment to a voice outside themselves expressing what is inside them? The silent ones appoint the speakers to deputize for them in an imaginary and forbidden parliament. People like direct poetry only in times of injustice, times of communal silence. Times when they are unable to speak or to act. Poetry that whispers and suggests can only be felt by free men. By the citizen who can speak up and does not have to give that task to another. I told myself our literary critics copy western theories with half-closed eyes and wear cowboy hats over their Arab skull-caps. (This metaphor of hats is a cliché, why does it come to me now?) And here is the first Israeli soldier—wearing a yarmulke. This is a real hat and not a literary conceit. His gun seems taller than him. He leans on the door of his solitary room on the west bank of the river, where the authority of the State of Israel begins. I can tell nothing of his feelings; his face shows nothing of his thoughts. I look at him as one looks at a closed door. Now my feet are on the west bank of the river. The bridge is behind me. I stand, a moment, on the dust, on earth. I am not a sailor with Columbus to cry out—when they were almost dead—"Land! Land! It's Land!" I am not Archimedes to cry out "Eureka!" I am not a victorious soldier kissing the earth. I did not kiss the earth. I was not sad and I did not weep.

But *his* image flickers in front of me in this pale wasteland; the image of his smile coming from over there, from his grave where I pillowed him with my own hand. In the darkness of that grave I embraced him for the last time and then the mourners pulled me away and I left him alone under the tombstone on which we had written: "Mounif 'Abd al-Razeq al-Barghouti, 1941–1993."

I walked a few steps.

I looked at the face of the soldier: for a moment he seemed a mere employee: bored and discontented. No. He is tense and alert (or is this my own state I project onto him?) Again no, it is a routine stance he takes every day as he sees thousands of Palestinians like me passing with their bags for a summer visit or leaving for Amman to get on with their lives. But my situation is different.

I said to myself, why does everyone in the world think that his particular situation is 'different'? Does a man want to be different even in loss? Is it an egotism that we cannot shake free of? Is it justified—since I am passing through here for the first time in thirty years? Those who lived under the Occupation were able to come and go across this bridge. So were the exiles who carried visiting permits or reunion permits. For thirty years I failed to get either. How would he know this? And why do I want him to know?

Last time, my spectacles were not so thick, and my hair was completely black. My memories were lighter, and my memory was better. Last time I was a boy. This time I am a father; the father of a boy who is as old as I was the last time I passed through here. Last time I passed through here I was leaving my country to go to a distant university. Now, I have left my son behind at that same university.

Last time no one argued my right to Ramallah, now I ask what I can do to preserve my son's right to see it. Shall I have him taken off the registers of the Refugees and the Displaced?—he never moved and never sought refuge. All he did was get born outside the homeland.

And now I pass from my exile to their . . . homeland? My homeland? The West Bank and Gaza? The Occupied Territories? The Areas? Judea and Samaria? The Autonomous Government? Israel? Palestine? Is there any other country in the world that so perplexes you with its names? Last time I was clear and things were clear. Now I am ambiguous and vague. Everything is ambiguous and vague.

This soldier with the yarmulke is not vague. At least his gun is very shiny. His gun is my personal history. It is the history of my estrangement. His gun took from us the land of the poem and left us with the poem of the land. In his hand he holds earth, and in our hands we hold a mirage.

But he is vague in another way. Did his parents come from Sachsenhausen or from Dachau? Or is he a settler newly arrived from Brooklyn? From Central Europe? North Africa? Latin America? Is he a dissident Russian émigré? Or was he born here and found himself here without ever wondering why he was here? Has he killed any of us in the wars of his State or in our continuous uprisings against his State? Can he develop an appetite for killing? Or is he performing a military duty he cannot avoid? Is there anyone who has tested his humanity? His own individual humanity? I know everything about the inhumanity of his job. He is a soldier of occupation, and in any case his situation is different from mine, especially at this moment. Can he notice my humanity? The humanity of the Palestinians who pass under the shadow of his shining gun every day?

We are here on the same bit of land, but he has no bag in his hand, and he stands between two Israeli flags that fly freely in the air and in international legitimacy.

"Wait here till the car comes."

He said it in Arabic.

"Where will the car take me?"

"To the border post. All the procedures are there."

I waited.

In his small room—which I had expected would be cleaner and more tidy—there were tourist posters depicting the beauties of . . . Israel! My eyes stopped at a poster of Massada. Their myth recounts that they had held fast in the fortress of Massada until they were all killed—but they did not surrender. Is this their message to us, they hang it on the gate to remind us that they will stay here forever? Was this a deliberate choice, or just a poster?

I look at the room: Two old chairs. A rectangular table. A mirror, the left corner of which is broken. Hebrew newspapers. A small kitchen and a rudimentary electric stove for tea and coffee. A standard guard's room, with the guard guarding our country— against us.

I thought he would interrogate me. He said nothing.

And even if he spoke to me, or asked me anything, would I have heard him? Or would I have turned a 'deaf ear?' And how could I have heard him when their voices have surrounded my silence since I sat on this chair? Those whom I saw coming through the door one after the other, to stand around me in this room, this bridge between two worlds; the world in which they took stands and felt joy and sorrow, and the world I shall soon see.

Would I have listened to him while the sound of their eternal silence fluttered here? Right here? In this place that they died far away from, were martyred before they reached?

The dead do not knock on the door. Enter my grandmother, the poet who lost her eyesight in old age and who improvised her verses—sad or happy—at the weddings and funerals of the village. I hear her whispered prayers at dawn; prayers I never found in poetry or in prose; they were unique to her. I used to lift the edge of the quilt and listen to the music of her words. I would slip into bed next to her when she went back to sleep. I would ask her to repeat her magical prayer, then take its music with me into a warm sleep. The music would stay with me in class; ring on the pages of my schoolbooks and turn the boredom of multiplication tables into the first enemy of my childhood.

Enter my father: from a grave I left behind me in Bayadir Wadi al-Sayr in Amman. He comes with his quiet tenderness, his narrow eyes, and his calm: bruised by the world and contented with it at the same time.

Enter Mounif who was laid waste by death: they ruined the beauty of his heart and of his intentions. They destroyed forever his dream of seeing Ramallah—if only for a few days.

Enter Ghassan Kanafani, whose voice could be silenced by nothing less than a bomb, an explosion that shook the whole of Hazimiya.

Would I have listened to this green soldier while Ghassan plunged the insulin syringe into his arm and produced a welcoming smile for Radwa and me in his office? Only on the posters covering the wall behind his shoulders was there thunder and lightning.

The posters of that time that was so unlike this. The star on Guevara's beret. The questions on Lenin's brow. Embroidery with the pen and the brush for the stolen name. A boundless horse, bounded in a frame. Photographs of the leaders of liberation movements in Asia and Africa and Latin America, slogans and images and writings we thought would lead to Palestine.

I wonder, is Ghassan closer now or farther from Acre?

I compare the posters in the room of this teenage soldier with the posters in Ghassan's office in Beirut. Opposed worlds: in Ghassan's world there was room for the poems of Neruda, the words of Cabral, Lenin's outstretched hand, and the vision of Fanon and the personal colors with which a novelist tries to paint the dream: in navy blue and apricot and orange, and with everything the rainbow may suggest to a narrow, gloomy sky full of omens of disaster and loss. And here? I look at the walls and the drawings. They are scenes from my country. But their context and their reason for being in this place at the forbidden border are aggressive. I remember the big picture that Naji al-'Ali gave me.

He asked Radwa and me to dinner at the Miami Restaurant on the beach in Beirut. At the end of the evening he got the picture out of the car: "This is what they printed with your poem in *al-Safir*. I drew it again—bigger. For you and Radwa and Tamim."

Then he drove off to his house in Sidon, and Radwa and I returned to our room at the Beau Rivage.

A child's face fills the center of the drawing. Her braids stick out horizontally: one to the right, the other to the left. The braids have turned into barbed wire, reaching to the edges of the drawing, against a very dark sky.

Enter Naji al-'Ali from his old death, his death that is still fresh. This is the smile in his eyes and this is his thin body. I listen to the cry that broke from my chest as I stood in front of his grave in a London suburb. I whispered—as I looked at the mound of dust— one word: "No!"

I said it in a whisper. Nobody heard it, not even nine-year-old Usama, who stood in front of me, my arm around his shoulders, both of us staring at his father's grave. But I could not regain the silence.

That 'no' refused to end.

It grew.

It rose.

I am wailing: one long, continuous wail.

I cannot pluck it back from the air, it hangs there, in that drizzle that fell on all of us together: on Usama and Judy and Layal and Khalid and Widad and me. As though it meant to stay in the sky until the Day of Judgment. That distant sky, not white, not blue, not ours, not . . . .

Widad's brother held my shoulders tight. I heard him say: "For God's sake, Mourid. Calm down, my brother. Calm down, so that we can stay on our feet."

I pulled myself back from the wail that had turned into a semi-swoon. I closed my mouth with my hand and after a while I found myself saying, my voice weak: "He's the one who's standing. Not us!"

We returned from his grave to his house in Wimbledon.

His family insisted that I should stay in his room. I slept among his unfinished drawings, his sketches. I saw his chair and his desk raised on a wooden platform he had made himself. A platform that raised his desk so that it was on a level with the window looking out on gardens and skies. The window had no curtains, the glass faced the world unprotected. Widad said she had made a curtain for it but Naji had taken it down because he "loves space" and felt that the curtain stifled him. The darkness of his grave leapt to my ear as I heard her describe his love of space.

In that room of his, I spent a week with the family. At his small desk, on his blank paper, with one of his pens, I wrote something about him. About his life and his drawings and his death. A poem I named "The Wolf Ate Him Up"; the title of one of his most famous drawings. I read it later at the opening of an exhibition of his works, organized by the Iraqi artist Dia al-'Azzawi and other friends in one of London's galleries.

At the door of the gallery three young men lined up to greet the guests arriving for the memorial service and the exhibition:

Khalid, son of the martyr Naji al-'Ali.

Fayiz, son of the martyr Ghassan Kanafani.

Hani, son of the martyr Wadi' Haddad.

All in the full bloom of youth. My mouth was dry as I embraced them at the entrance to the gallery. What funerals brought forward these high shoulders and these alert, intelligent eyes? What ruins did their childhood mature in to emerge now into manhood, unlicensed by the murderers?

Khalid presented his two friends to me and I greeted them. I wanted to hear their voices, their tones.

They seemed to me that night as though they were in a scene in a novel rather than in real life. I said to myself as I watched them stand in a row to receive the guests: in our traditions, the men who stood like this to receive those who come to condole or congratulate were the notables of the families or of the political factions (for factions have their notables too). Today, these young men put forward their new definition—fresh and wonderful—of 'notable.' That word which—before them—I could not stand.

I went back to Budapest trembling at the shape of our days to come, leaving under the distant British earth one of the bravest artists in the whole of Palestinian history.

Their faces swam around me as though they were icons of Andre Rublyev, glimmering in dark temples in the thirteenth century. The armed guard's room was not dark, neither was the emptiness outside his room. I have never felt a day as hot as this. Or is it the beginning of a fever creeping up on me? Abu Salma entered and so did Mu'in and Kamal, and with them the poetry of their hearts that were bigger than their papers. Mounif and Naji came back a second time, and a third, and tension once again filled the room. Faces, fantasies, voices appear and disapear. I look at the glance. I call to the voice. Completely with you. Completely alone. May your darkness forgive me this particular day, my friends!

Is all this confusion mine? The absent are so present—and so absent. This ennui surrounded by the salt of the Dead Sea.

I am used to waiting. I have not entered any Arab country easily, and today too I will not enter easily.

The car arrived.

I walked toward it slowly.

A tall driver, fair-skinned, he wears a shirt with the buttons undone. It seemed to me he said something in Arabic. He did not speak much, otherwise I would have found out if he was an Arab or an Israeli. Things are getting confused. We used to read about the Arab workers in Israel. Is he an 'Arab worker in Israel'? Is he an Israeli who knows Arabic?

My questioning did not last long; we arrived at the border post.

He took his fare in Jordanian dinars.

I entered a large hall, like the arrivals hall in an airport, and here I saw the Palestinian police and the Israeli police.

A row of windows to deal with people going to the West Bank, and those going to Gaza.

So many people.

The hall led to a narrow electronic gate. The Israeli police asked me to put any metal objects—watch, keys, and some coins—into a plastic dish.

I passed through the gate and found myself facing an armed Israeli officer. He stopped me, asked for my papers, looked through them, and returned them.

In an attempt to deal with my own tension I decided to be the first to ask a question: "Where do I go now?"

"To the Palestinian officer, of course."

He motioned toward a room nearby.

The Palestinian officer takes my papers and turns them over in his hands then gives them back to the same Israeli officer, who smiles in a deliberate fashion and asks me to wait. I ask him, where?

"With the Palestinian officer, of course."

I sit in the room. The Palestinian officer comes and goes and pays me no attention.

I was abstracted. The officer sat silently at his table. There were two of us in that room, and each one was alone.

In that room I found myself retreating to 'there'; to that hidden place inside each one of us, the place of silence and introspection. A dark, private space in which I take refuge when the outside world becomes absurd or incomprehensible. As though I have a secret curtain at my command: I draw it when I need to, and screen my inner world against the outer one. Drawing it is quick and automatic when my thoughts and observations become too difficult to understand clearly, when screening them is the only way to preserve them.

I entered that empty space in which there is no room for conversation with others. I did not concern myself for long with the odd situation of the man. It was clear that the Agreements had placed him in a position in which he could make no decisions. All security, customs, and administration procedures were their business, the business of 'the other side.'

After about an hour one of their officers appeared; a different officer.

He took me to a room in which there was a man in civilian clothes. He had a printed form in front of him and his questions were of a statistical nature. He did not ask any political questions. He was opening a file for me.

"Go now and identify your bag."

Another wait for the arrival of the bag on the conveyor belt.

A hall crowded with those who had crossed the bridge and who—like me—were waiting for their bags. And on the right a room where chosen bags were searched. Cardboard boxes, domestic appliances, televisions and refrigerators, fans, woolen blankets. Bedding and bundles and bags of every shape and size. When I travel I take with me the smallest and lightest bag possible. I do not like what luggage does to a traveler. And I hate having to open my bag and display its contents to an officer looking for something I am ignorant of.

Israeli men and women wearing nylon gloves and searching the contents of the bags filling the room; the owners of the bags waiting for their possessions.

A blonde Israeli girl conscript lazily matches the numbers of the bags registered on her computer to the number pasted into the passport. I give her my passport, pointing out that all I have is one bag and that I can see it among the bags in the middle of the hall. Yet she asks me to wait.

After a short while she motions to me to go into the luggage hall.

I pick up my small bag. I pass through the huge gate.

I leave the whole building for the road . . . .

The gate of gates,
No key in our hand. But we entered,
Refugees to our birth from the strange death
And refugees to our homes that were our homes and we came.
In our joys there were scratches
Unseen by tears until they're about to flow.

I walk two steps and stop.

Here I stand, with my feet upon this dust. Mounif did not reach this point. A coldness runs through my spine. Relief is not complete. Desolation is not complete.

The gates of exile were opened to us from a strange direction!

The direction that leads to *the* country and not to the countries of others.

I stand on the dust of this land. On the earth of this land.

My country carries me.

Palestine at this moment is not the golden map hanging on a golden chain adorning the throats of women in exile. I used to wonder—every time I saw that map encircling their necks—if Canadian women, or Norwegians, or Chinese carried their maps around their necks as our women do.

I said once to a friend: "When Palestine is no longer a chain worn with an evening dress, an ornament or a memory or a golden Qur'an, when we walk on Palestinian dust, and wipe it off our shirt collars and off our shoes, hurrying to conduct our daily affairs—our passing, normal, boring affairs—when we grumble about the heat in Palestine and the dullness of staying there too long, then we will really have come close to it."

Here it is now in front of you, you who are journeying toward it. Look at it well.

On the pavement opposite the building I meet the first Palestinian performing a clear and understandable function: a thin, elderly man sits at a small table that he has set up in the shade of a wall. He seeks shelter from the June heat. He calls to me in a loud voice: "Come here, brother. Take a bus ticket."

There is nothing more lonely than to be called to in this way. 'Brother' is specifically that phrase that cancels out brotherhood. I looked at him for a moment.

I paid for the ticket in Jordanian money. I moved away two or three steps, then stopped. I turned to him again—then ran for the bus. No. I did not exactly run. I walked entirely normally.

Something inside me was running. I sat in the bus until it filled up with others like me who had crossed the bridge. I asked the driver where we were going now.

"To the Jericho resthouse."

Here I am, entering Palestine at last. But what are all these Israeli flags?

I look out of the bus window and I see their flags appearing and disappearing at the repeated checkpoints. Every few meters their flags appear.

A feeling of depression I do not want to admit to. A feeling of security refusing to become complete.

My eyes do not leave the window. And images of times past and ended do not leave my eyes.

On this slow bus I recall as though I had been there yesterday the breakfast room in the Caravan Hotel where we met as family for the first time after '67.

That was in the summer after the war, the summer of 1968. I was working in Kuwait. My mother and my youngest brother, 'Alaa, were in Ramallah. My father was in Amman and Majid was at the Jordanian University. Mounif was working in Qatar.

Across all the methods of communication available to us in those days, we agreed to meet in Amman. We arrived, one after another, at the Caravan Hotel in Jebel al-Luwaybda; a small, elegant hotel of three or four stories.

This was my first meeting with my mother and father and brothers since war separated us. We took three rooms side by side. Hotels are made for sleeping. We did not sleep. Morning surprised us as though it was not agreed upon in the solar system, as though it came and went without logic and without being expected.

I have never tasted a breakfast like the breakfasts of that summer.

Wonderful to start your day with the whole family after all those strange months. We would look at one another as though each one were discovering the presence of the others for the first time in that place. As though each day we recaptured the motherhood of our mother and the fatherhood of our father, the brotherhood of brothers and ourselves as sons. The strange thing is that none of us spoke of these feelings. Our joy in being together in that hotel hung in the air around us. We felt it and did not wish to make it explicit. As though it were a secret. As though we were all required to suppress it.

The hotel itself, the idea of the hotel, implied the certainty that this was a transient meeting, passing, and nearing its end. From the first night the meeting turned to terror of the certain parting. Tension mingled with happiness. We could not agree if we should order the salad with olive oil or without; one wanted it chopped small, the other large.

The greatest tension showed when we were trying to decide on small expeditions : one suggested a visit to some relatives living in Amman, another did not want to go out at all, and a third suggested some other destination. But there was fun, and there were jokes, none of which I can remember though I remember the atmosphere so clearly.

In the Caravan Hotel I got to know my brothers and my parents all over again. For everyone there were new and exceptional circumstances I could not know completely. And for me there were others. My uncle 'Ata, with an insistence not to be resisted, had more or less made me go to Kuwait, and there I had found work in the technical college, for it was unthinkable that Mounif should carry on supporting me after I had graduated. I have never liked teaching. I took the job as a temporary measure until things became clearer.

Since '67 everything we do is temporary 'until things become clearer.' And things are no clearer now after thirty years. Even what I am doing now is not clear to me. I am impelled toward it and I do not judge my impulse. Would it be an impulse if we judged it?

In the disaster of 1948 the refugees found shelter in neighboring countries as a 'temporary' measure. They left their food cooking on stoves, thinking to return in a few hours. They scattered in tents and camps of zinc and tin 'temporarily.' The commandos took arms and fought from Amman 'temporarily,' then from Beirut 'temporarily,' then they moved to Tunis and Damascus 'temporarily.' We drew up interim programs for liberation 'temporarily' and they told us they had accepted the Oslo Agreements 'temporarily,' and so on, and so on. Each one said to himself and to others 'until things become clearer.'

Young 'Alaa pleads to join his father and brothers. My father is not allowed—as a soldier in the Jordanian army—to go to the West Bank after the Occupation.

My mother wants to plan the life of the family in circumstances that make the idea of planning absurd. She is absorbed in working out alternatives.

Her desire to defy difficulty and fragmentation is so powerful it paints her tired face with a new vitality. Her green eyes, almost triangular, shine with alertness even at the peak of drowsiness in the small hours of the morning.

My father's tranquility makes you think that things will work out in the end even if one does nothing to help them along. Something of the patience of the wise men of India colors his calmness; a calmness that irritates my mother, who is always questing, scratching for solutions with her fingernails.

His narrow eyes, black, do not reveal his heart except when he laughs. I am the only one who has inherited the blackness of his eyes and their narrowness. Mounif, Majid, and 'Alaa all have green eyes like my mother. Mounif, a young man of striking good looks, who plays the part of a parent to his younger brothers at twenty-seven. Every problem he volunteers to solve and every sacrifice he hastens to make, simply and without hesitation.

Majid, always tall, has grown taller. He has a way of drawing mirth even out of tragedy. He paints and sculpts and writes poetry that he does not wish to publish (until now he will not publish, even though what he writes is remarkable). He has an alert, attentive heart.

Young 'Alaa, who loves philosophy. He wants to study engineering. He writes songs in the local dialect and wants to learn to play the lute. His fair face and African hair give him an individual handsomeness. 'Alaa has kept alive a child in himself, rare for a man whose hair is turning white.

The scattering of the family taught it to stick together. And when we meet, we four men become once again the children of our parents, no matter that we have become the fathers of their grandchildren.

After two weeks each one of us went back to his place.

We agreed that my mother would live with my father and Majid and 'Alaa in Amman for some time, then go back to Ramallah to renew her permit and identity papers so that she would not lose her right to live in—the now completely occupied—Palestine.

The right to citizenship even under occupation was something to be held on to, whatever the circumstances. My mother still carries her identity card and she is still a citizen of the Occupied Territories. But they never allowed her to get a reunion permit for Mounif or for me.

We did not meet as a whole family again until ten years later in Doha when we visited Mounif before he left Qatar for France.

I was surprised by the bus stopping, as though it had arrived ahead of time. The porters were yelling under the windows. I remembered how short the distances were in Palestine.

I took my bag and got off the bus.

This is the Jericho resthouse.

Here, the arrivals are distributed to the different towns.

Here, there are only Palestinian flags.

Taxicabs queue under signposts bearing the names of cities: Ramallah, Nablus, Jenin, Tulkarm, al-Khalil, Gaza, and Jerusalem.

As in every station you are met by the drivers quarreling over fares: shouts, threats, shoves. A young Palestinian policeman appears and quietly breaks up the fight.

The car moves toward Ramallah.

I sit next to the driver in an old Mercedes carrying seven passengers.

In the car I am mute. Or am I chattering my life? Have I been struck by my life as a man is struck by a fever?—you think him asleep and silent while his whole body is telling stories.

These are my people. Why do I not talk with them?

I used to tell my Egyptian friends at university that Palestine was green and covered with trees and shrubs and wild flowers. What are these hills? Bare and chalky. Had I been lying to people, then? Or has Israel changed the route to the bridge and exchanged it for this dull road that I do not remember ever seeing in my childhood?

Did I paint for strangers an ideal picture of Palestine because I had lost it? I said to myself, when Tamim comes here he will think I have been describing another country.

I wanted to ask the driver if the road had been like this for many years, but I did not. I had a lump in my throat and a feeling of being let down.

Had I been describing Deir Ghassanah with its surrounding olive groves, and convincing myself I was describing the whole country? Or was I describing Ramallah, the beautiful, lush, summer resort and thinking that each spot in Palestine was exactly like it?

Did I really know a great deal about the Palestinian countryside? The car moves on and I continue to look out of the windows to my right and to the left of the driver. What is this Israeli flag? We entered our 'areas' a while ago. These, then, are the settlements.

Statistics are meaningless. Discussions and speeches and proposals and condemnations and reasons and maps for negotiation and the excuses of negotiators and all we have heard and read about the settlements, all this is worth nothing. You have to see them for yourself.

Buildings of white stone standing together on a stepped incline. One behind the other in neat rows. Solid where they stand. Some are apartment blocks and some are houses with tiled roofs. This is what the eye sees from a distance.

I wonder what their lives look like on the inside?

Who lives in this settlement? Where were they before they were brought here? Do their kids play football behind those walls? Do their men and women make love behind those windows? Do they make love with guns strapped to their sides? Do they hang loaded machine guns ready on their bedroom walls?

On television we only ever see them armed.

Are they really afraid of us, or is it we who are afraid?

If you hear a speaker on some platform use the phrase 'dismantling the settlements,' then laugh to your heart's content. These are not children's fortresses of Lego or Meccano. These are Israel itself; Israel the idea and the ideology and the geography and the trick and the excuse. It is the place that is ours and that they have made theirs. The settlements are their book, their first form. They are our absence. The settlements are the Palestinian Diaspora itself.

I said to myself that the negotiators of Oslo were ignorant of the true meaning of these settlements, otherwise they would never have signed the Agreement.

You look out of the car window on your right and are surprised to find that the narrow, worn strip that carries you has turned into a wide, smooth elegant road. The asphalt shines, and soon it separates out, rising to a hill with classy buildings, and you realize it leads to a settlement.

After a while you look out to your left and you see another settlement and another good, wide road leading up to it. Then you see a third and a fourth and a tenth, and so on.

Israeli flags rise at the entrances, and the signposts are in Hebrew. Who built all this?

When I crossed the bridge, the leader of the Likud, Benyamin Netanyahu, was waiting for the final results that would confirm that he had won the elections. It is the Labor Party then.

Since the time of Ben Gurion, the Labor Party has been building these settlements on our land. The fools of the Likud make a lot of noise about their settlement policy and about each new settlement they build. But the brains of the Labor Party remind me of a story I read long ago about a thief who stole a car:

He returned it to its owners the next day and left them—inside it—a polite note of apology. He said he had not meant to steal their car, he had just needed it for one night to go out with his sweetheart. And he is returning the car, with two theater tickets, in apology and to show his goodwill.

The owners smiled and admired the sensitivity of the lover/thief and his good manners.

In the evening they went to the theater.

They returned late at night to find everything of value stolen from their home.

A killer can strangle you with a silk scarf, or can smash your head in with an axe; in both cases you are dead.

The symmetry is not absolute, of course, between the story of the Labor Party and the story of the thief. But the duality of intelligence and stupidity has been part of the Zionist project from the beginning. And there are always, in Israel, representatives of both.

And in any case they are the winners. They gain from smooth deliberation, and from strong-arm tactics.

Moderates, at one time or another, learn a new language from extremists. And the extremists—if they have to—will learn from the moderates how to speak with silken tongues. And we, the owners of the house, lose in any case and in every way.

How did we let them build all these cities? These fortresses? These barracks? Year after year?

Bashir al-Barghouti told me, several years ago, that from the balcony of his house in Deir Ghassanah he could see the lights of the settlements proliferating year after year until they encircled the village. They had gradually, and in the shade of our long silence, spread everywhere.

The weave of the carpet is the settlements. Some scattered figures here and there are all that is left to us of Palestine. In the terms of the (last) negotiations they left our houses, but they continue to occupy the roads leading to them. They can stop you at any of the numerous checkpoints and you have to obey.

As for Jerusalem, I was not allowed to enter it or see it. Even the road to Ramallah that used to go by Jerusalem they changed via a complex of winding roads so that we may not see the city even from the car window.

Only in the company of a Palestinian leader carrying a VIP card can you go to Jerusalem. (And nobody with a VIP card issued by the Israelis will take you to visit Jerusalem unless you are a VIP for him). I found no one to take me to Jerusalem.

When we arrived at al-Sharafa Square I asked the driver if he knew the house of Dr. Hilmi al-Muhtadi. He said: "But he died years ago."

"I know."

(I did not know. But Abu Hazim had described his house to me as 'opposite the house of Dr. Hilmi al-Muhtadi.')

I added: "I'm going to a house nearby."

Abu Hazim used to live—like us—in the Liftawi Building, but he had moved. And in spite of the careful directions he had given me—and before me Mounif—I was so distracted and tense that I could not remember what he had said. And I had arrived in Ramallah after dark.

The driver said: "I know his clinic at al-Manara, but I don't know the house."

The lady sitting in the back asked me exactly which house I was looking for.

"The house of Mughira al-Barghouti, Abu Hazim."

She asked me the name of his wife.

I said:

"Fadwa al-Barghouti. She works in the In'ash al-Usra Society."

She said she knew her and had worked with her, but she did not know the house.

Another passenger from the back seat said to the driver:

"Try taking the next left then ask. I think the doctor's house is close to here."

The driver turned left and then stopped in the hope that a passer-

32

by could tell us the way. It was 8:30 pm. But the moment he stopped, I heard voices calling:

"*'Ammu* Mourid, *'Ammu* Mourid. Come up. We're here!"

In a second they were around me.

"Where's your father?"

Fadwa said that the moment he had seen one of the bridge cars stopping (with the luggage on top) he had gone to the phone to call my mother in Amman.

I knew that my mother would have spent the whole day by the phone until she heard I had arrived safely. The experience of getting Mounif back from the bridge is still constantly with her. And when she said goodbye to me on the bridge her face was a mixture of hope and despair.

I knew also that Radwa and Tamim in Cairo had been waiting since noon for me to contact them from Ramallah.

"We've all been on the balconies since noon."

And her daughter, Abeer, said: "Watchtowers. Father and mother on the first floor balconies, Sam and I on the second. Praise God for your safe arrival."

Abu Hazim went for me with open arms.

He went for me with his white hair and outstretched arms: a running cross. A happy cross running toward me. Our shoulders met two-thirds of the way to his house.

I called my mother and 'Alaa and Elham in Amman, and Radwa and Tamim in Cairo: "I'm in Ramallah."

And on Abu Hazim's balcony there it was, in its black frame, hanging on the wall, the first thing my eyes fell upon: Mounif's photograph.

33

2

THIS IS RAMALLAH

The first morning in Ramallah. I wake up and hasten to open the window.

"What are these elegant houses, Abu Hazim?" I asked, pointing at Jabal al-Tawil, which overlooks Ramallah and Bireh.

"A settlement."

Then he added: "Tea? Coffee? Breakfast is ready."

What a beginning to my resumed relationship with the homeland! Politics confront me at every turn. But in Ramallah and Bireh there are things other than the settlements.

Returning to the city of your childhood and your youth after thirty years you try to coax joy to your heart as you would coax chickens to their barley. Why is it that your joy has to be coaxed and persuaded? That it will not simply manifest itself strong and clear? Is it because there is something incomplete about the whole scene? Something missing from the promise, and from what is fulfilled of the promise? Is it because you are burdened? Because you are not yet used to familiarity? Are you in the dance or sitting it out? Are your objections to the music or to the musicians?

Joy needs training and experience. You have to take the first step. Ramallah will not take it. Ramallah is content with what she is. She knows what she has lived through. The near ones are near and the far ones are far. She has gone her way, sometimes as her people willed, and more often as her enemies willed. She has suffered and she has endured. Is she waiting to rest her head on your shoulder or is it you who seeks refuge in her strength?

A confused meeting. It is unclear who is giving and who is taking. You used to say that to your woman. Love is the confusion of roles between the giver and the taker. So we are speaking of love. Very well then: here are the chickens of joy responding to the spontaneous coaxing (is there such a thing as spontaneous coaxing?). You say take me to my school, to Shari' al-Iza'a, to the house of *Khali* Abu Fakhri, to the Liftawi Building. Take me to the home of *Hajja* Umm Isma'il, to houses I have lived in and paths I have trodden. Here you are: treading them again—as Mounif could not. Mounif, who lies now in his grave on the edge of Amman. Being forbidden to return killed him. Three years ago they sent him back from the bridge after a day of waiting. He tried again a few months later and they sent him back a second time. My mother, three years after the event, cannot forget her last moments with him on the bridge. He was desperate to get back into the Palestine that he had left when he was just eighteen years old.

Someone should write about the role of the older brother in the Palestinian family. From his adolescence he is afflicted with the role of brother and father and mother and head of family and dispenser of advice. He is the child who has always to prefer others to himself. The child who gives and does not acquire. The child who keeps watch over a flock both older and younger and so excels at noticing things.

His sudden death was the great deafening collapse in the lives of the whole family. He had arrived at this final gate but it had not opened for him.

Here I step on a patch of earth that his feet will never reach. But the mirror in the waiting room reflected his face when I looked into it. The streets of Ramallah, when I walked in them, saw him walk, hurrying, leading with his chest. Since I handed my papers in to the Bridge Authorities, his face has been with me. This scene is his. It is Mounif's scene.

Here he waited. Here he felt afraid. Here he had a surge of optimism. Here they questioned him. Here they allowed my mother to enter, and forbade him. Here they had to part. She, forced to continue her journey west toward Ramallah, he east toward Amman and from there to his French exile, where six months later he died. He was not yet fifty-two. Here she screamed at the soldiers: "Then let me go back with him." Here she wept on his shoulder, and he wept on hers. Here she said goodbye to him for the last time.

When I entered Deir Ghassanah his hand was in mine; we walked side by side to Dar Ra'd, our old house. And when I crossed the threshold for the first time in thirty years, the tremor that hit me was the same that took hold of me as I carried his body down into the grave on that dazed rainy day in a cemetery on the edge of Amman.

I have not been to Deir Ghassanah yet. They are preparing a meeting with the townspeople and a poetry reading. I am in Ramallah.

I entered by night. The road was long. In 1967 I started walking. From dawn yesterday to dawn today I have not stopped walking.

Here, the obstinate spring does not want to surrender to the shy, hesitant summer at the usual time. Spring shoves forward with its shoulders, its colors. With the chill, dew-laden gasp in its air. With its green, deliberately kept light—just short of the completion required by summer.

The chaos of cities, the quiet of the wild open spaces, the slogans of the young people of the Intifada, the distinctive smell of primary school. The taste of chalk. The voice of Ustaz Ahmad Salih 'Abd al-Hamid, and Ahmad Farhud and the clever student who can tell the specification from the attribute from the circumstance. And how to describe this circumstance that we have (not?) arrived at? And how to distinguish between ideologies and conflicting opinions and political theories on the one hand and this green fig that covers a third of the hill next to Abu Hazim's house on the other?

This window I am looking out of is some thirty years away; thirty years and nine volumes of verse. It is the distance of an eye from its tears under the willow of a distant graveyard. I look out of the window at my life, the only life that my mother gave me, at the life of those absent to the farthest point of absence. And why is it that in the window of joy I am overcome by the memory of elegies?

They are here. Do they look with me out of the window? Do they see what I see? Do I rejoice in what gives them joy, make fun of what they mock, object to what they object to? Can I write with their pens on their snow-white paper the things that come to my mind now that martyrs also are part of reality, and that the blood of the freedom fighters and the young people of the Intifada is also real. They are not invented by Walt Disney or born of the imagination of al-Manfaluti. Living people grow old but martyrs grow younger.

Ramallah of the cypresses and the pine trees. The swinging slopes of the hills, the green that speaks in twenty languages of beauty, our first schools where each one of us sees the other children bigger and stronger. The Teachers' College. The Hashemite. The Friends. Ramallah Secondary. Our guilty glances at the girls from the prep school swinging confidence in their right hands and confusion in their left and dazzling our minds when they look at us while pretending not to. Our small coffee-shops. Al-Manara Square. Abu Hazim told me that al-Manara was removed because of the new traffic system in the town center. They put traffic lights in its place. The graffiti. The flowers of the Intifada and its transparent steel, its traces clear as a lilac fingerprint.

After how many more thirty years will the ones who never came back return? What does my return, or the return of any other individual mean? It is their return, the return of the millions, that is the true return. Our dead are still in the cemeteries of others. Our living are clinging to foreign borders. On the bridge, that strange border unmatched on any of the world's five continents, you are overwhelmed by your memories of standing at the borders of others.

So what is new? The others are still masters of the place. They give you a permit. They check your papers. They start files on you. They make you wait. Am I hungry for my own borders? I hate borders, boundaries, limits. The boundaries of the body, of writing, of behavior, of states. Do I really want boundaries for Palestine? Will they necessarily be better boundaries?

It is not only the stranger who suffers at the border. Citizens too can have a bad time of it. There are no limits to the questions. No boundaries for the homeland. Now I want borders that later I will come to hate.

Ramallah is odd. Many cultures, many faces. Never a masculine or a solemn city. Always first to catch on to some new craze. In Ramallah I saw the *dabka* as though I were in Deir Ghassanah. And there, in my teenage years, I learned to tango. In al-Anqar billiard hall I learned to play snooker. In Ramallah I started to try my hand at poetry, and in the Walid and Dunya and Jamil cinemas I grew to love movies. In Ramallah I grew used to celebrating Christmas and the New Year.

We were never followed by curious eyes as we headed—girls and boys—for Rukab's garden café, where on white-pebbled paths in the shade of spreading trees we consumed chocolate mousse, peach melba, banana splits, and milk shakes.

In Ramallah Park, Bireh Park, and Na'um Park we stayed late into the night with our friends and our families. At the elegant tables of the 'Ouda Hotel and Harb Hotel we would recognize celebrities wearing fezzes and discussing politics while holding the long tubes of the narghiles. The streets and restaurants and parks of Ramallah and its twin city, al-Bireh, were sparkling clean.

And in Ramallah I came to know demonstrations for the first time in my life. We demonstrated against the Baghdad Pact, as did the people of Jerusalem and Nablus and other cities. While we were still in short trousers we were shaken by the news of the martyrdom of our fellow student Raja Abu 'Amasha in those demonstrations. I knew that Mounif hid illegal pamphlets in his shoes, that because he was a child he could transport them from one place to another without arousing suspicion. We followed the news of the arrest of our cousin, Basheer, and visited his mother, our neighbor in the Liftawi Building, to console her and find out his news.

We demonstrated in support of firing Glubb Pasha and Arabizing the Jordanian army, and we danced for joy when—as a result of later political developments—these things happened. With the minds of teenagers we followed the conflicts between the political parties: the Communists, the Ba'th, and the Muslim Brotherhood. We followed the elections that brought in the government of Sulayman al-Nabulsi. We listened in secret to the speeches of Gamal 'Abd al-Nasser on the Voice of the Arabs—in secret because listening to that station was enough to arouse suspicion and get you questioned.

And in Ramallah we rejoiced at Nasser's decision to nationalize the Suez Canal, and we followed the news of the war in Port Said and the city's resistance. And in Ramallah we celebrated the union between Egypt and Syria and the birth of the United Arab Republic, and there we wept when the union was dissolved. In Ramallah we were caressed by al-Qahir and al-Zafir missiles into dreams of power, and we heard for the first time of the 'socialist' resolutions coming out of Egypt and wondered, we young schoolchildren, about the meaning of the term.

We woke up to the voice of Abu al-Habayib, the newspaper seller, who—summer or winter—never took off the British army overcoat that was too long for him so that its hem dragged on all the streets of Ramallah: *"Al-Difa'! Al-Jihad! Filasteen!"* All three newspapers stopped coming out later. As for Abu al-Habayib it was his fate to be killed by shrapnel in front of our house, the Liftawi Building. They found his body on that grim morning in June 1967, his face and his long coat covered by the newspapers whose names he had spent his life announcing in the streets. Where had Abu al-Habayib come from? Where were his people? Everybody knew him and nobody knew him. He was hit by shrapnel after he had been hit by displacement in the Ramallah that he had never left. Was he a citizen or a stranger? Who could explain the difference to you, newspaper-seller? And what killed you? The shrapnel or the headlines?

How can we explain today, now that we have grown older and wiser, that we on the West Bank treated our people as refugees? Yes, our own people, banished by Israel from their coastal cities and villages in 1948, our people who had to move from one part of the homeland to another and came to live in our cities and towns, we called them refugees! We called them immigrants! Who can apologize to them? Who can apologize to us? Who can explain this great confusion to whom? Even in a small village like Deir Ghassanah, we heard—in our childhood—words like 'immigrants' and 'refugees.'

We were familiar with these words, comfortable using them. How is it that we did not ask ourselves then about their meaning? How is it that the adults did not scold us for using them?

The wish to count the faults of the victim has woken in me once again; it is not enough to register the faults of others, the Occupier, the Colonialist, the Imperialist, and so on. Disasters do not fall on people's heads like comets from the sky on a beautiful natural scene. We too have our faults; our share of shortsightedness. I am certain that we were not always a beautiful natural scene. But this truth does not absolve the enemy of his original crime that is the beginning and the end of this evil. I know that it is the easiest thing to stare at the faults of others and that if you look for faults you see little else. Which is why—after each setback that befalls us—I look for our faults too; the faults of our song. I ask if my attachment to the homeland can reach a sophistication that is reflected in my song for it. Does a poet live in space or in time? Our homeland is the shape of the time we spent in it. Perhaps I am ill-intentioned. I only believed a little of what Nazim Hikmat had to say. My troubles in exile were no worse than the troubles of my friends in their home-lands. I cannot stand a fraudulent yearning.

Am I uncomfortable with the concept of singing for a concept? Is that why I look at a poem as structure rather than song? I cannot even speak to a girlfriend with the common and expected romanticism and I generally do not make friends with men or women who do not take the first steps toward me. I can easily turn my back on a relationship if I find it tiresome. A tiresome friend is full of reproaches, full of blame, wanting an explanation for the inexplicable, wanting to understand everything. If he forgives you for a mistake he makes you feel he's forgiven you for a mistake. We do not choose our families but we do choose our friends, so, in my view, a tiresome friendship is a voluntary stupidity.

I also do not find it easy to fit in with any grouping. I was never convinced enough to join any political party and I have never joined any faction of the Palestine Liberation Organization. Perhaps, for someone who has lost his country, that is a vice rather than a virtue.

Not only that. I have resisted open and implicit invitations from those factions and parties. And I have paid varying prices for my abstention. The interesting thing is that they approach you because they find you deserving and different and see in you characteristics that please them. They hint that they need you and that they want you 'with them.' You thank them for their good opinion and for their generosity that manifests itself in their noticing an unimportant person like yourself. Then you explain how you prefer to act independently of any organizations or parties; that you prefer to remain faithful to what you perceive as your nature. Here, and in an immediate and sudden fashion, they start to deal with you exactly as though you were their enemy, or as someone of absolutely no value.

I have personal friends of all political persuasions who have realized that I do not understand the concept of 'unconditional support.' I believe in my right to 'elect,' starting with the right to elect a kilogram of tomatoes with my own hand at the greengrocer's, to my right to elect my government or the representative who speaks in my name. I cannot condone every decision of the 'tribe.' I do not measure behavior by right and wrong, nor by what is 'permitted' and what is 'sinful.' My measure is aesthetic. There are things that are right and ugly and that I will not do and will not follow even though I have the right. And there are beautiful mistakes I do not hesitate to make impulsively and contentedly. But—

There is that which always mars contentment.
What is it that before its beginnings are established
Comes to an end!

Where does this small lump in the throat and the mind come from, while I am inside the dream itself? I have not exactly 'returned.' And so we return to politics. Can the defeated be let off politics? Can they be distanced from it? How can our Arab francophone and anglophone critics believe this? No one has defined art properly for them, or politics for that matter. They speak of politics as 'facts.' As though no one had explained to them the difference between 'facts' and that 'reality' which includes all the emotions of people and their positions. And which includes also triangular time (the past of moments, their present, and their future). They speak of politics as the decisions of governments and parties and states, like the eight o'clock news.

Politics is the family at breakfast. Who is there and who is absent and why. Who misses whom when the coffee is poured into the waiting cups. Can you, for example, afford your breakfast? Where are your children who have gone forever from these their usual chairs? Whom do you long for this morning? What rhythm is it that pushes you to hurry toward pleasures life has promised you,

43

or to a confrontation you wish you could win just this once? Where are the children of this mother who, in her slightly crooked spectacles, sits knitting a pullover of dark blue wool for the absent one who does not write regularly? Where is your gentle chatter, your splendid isolation, your lack of need of the outside world for even a few moments? Where is your illusion laid bare by the newspaper lying on the cane chair at your side? What small act of forgiveness are you training yourself to perform today? What reproach do you wish to utter? And what reproach do you wish erased? Who threatens your wonderful mistakes, staying up to spoil your night? Who ruins your sweet inconsequential things with the awe of his authority and his driver and his servants and his happy bodyguards? Who imported this small, shiny teaspoon from Taiwan? What giant ships ploughed the seas to bring you some trivial piece of primitive gadgetry from Stockholm? How did the flower merchants make their millions and build their fine houses from selling the bouquets carried by mothers and sisters to the graveyards that are always damp: raindrops, flowers, and tears. You question why even the silence in the graveyards is wet. Politics is the number of coffee-cups on the table, it is the sudden presence of what you have forgotten, the memories you are afraid to look at too closely, though you look anyway. Staying away from politics is also politics. Politics is nothing and it is everything.

"No, without sugar, Abu Hazim. I might be hungry later."

Three years ago he said to Mounif: "The veranda is ready to receive you, Abu Ghassan."

He swore he would not allow Mounif or me to stay anywhere but at his house if we were ever permitted to visit the homeland. Here is Mounif's photograph in its black frame hanging on the veranda. I think of Ghassan and Ghada and Ghadeer, Mounif's chil-

dren who are still displaced. Displaced by his absence from them
and their absence from here. Will they accept my care for them after
him? Is there a place in their lives for an uncle who writes poetry?
How well do they know me, I wonder? They will propose the
'place' that they wish me and Majid and 'Alaa and my mother to
occupy in their lives. Life has taught me that we have to love people in the way that they want us to love them. I said to them, as soon
as I could say anything after the death of their father: "Think of me
as a dictionary in your house that you pick up when you need it."

I asked Fadwa what time she went to work; she said she was on holiday for a week. I realized she had done this for me and I was
touched by the generous gesture. I tried to persuade her to go back
to work and she promised she would—after a few days—and
changed the subject.

"Umm Khalil is very glad you're here. She'll come to see you
tonight or tomorrow."

"Does Umm Khalil run your organization better than 'Arafat
runs the PLO?" I joked.

"Umm Khalil is just fine," she smiled.

"How do you get the newspapers, Abu Hazim?" I asked. "I'd
like to see our papers."

"Well. Sometimes they have things in them. One has to see them."

Husam came in with sesame bread and thyme cakes.

"Mourid won't have breakfast. He's giving me a hard time. You
tell him."

Husam will take me to the Palestinian Home Office to apply for
an identity card. And also for an entry permit for Tamim.

After a while Anis came in carrying a third breakfast: Hummus
and stewed beans, and sesame cakes too.

"You want your tea in a cup or in a glass, Abu al-Uns?" Abu Hazim asked him. He was trying not to laugh but throwing me the mischievous glances of someone threatening to reveal a long-forgotten secret. I burst out laughing and so did Fadwa and then Abu Hazim himself, while Husam and Anis looked at us in surprise. We did not explain to them the incident behind our laughter.

It happened that my school, Ramallah Secondary School, held a literary competition when I was in the third form, and I won first prize. Abu Hazim came with me to the award-giving ceremony in the Great Hall of the Hashimiya School, where they handed out the prizes for the competition and for the top students in the various academic subjects, sports, and so on.

Each student went up to the stage, shook hands with the headmaster and received his prize: a Parker pen or a small leather briefcase, some books, a watch.

My name was called, I went up, the headmaster shook my hand, but instead of handing me my prize he pointed to a large cardboard box on the stage. As I went to the box Abu Hazim shot up from the auditorium and clambered up on to the stage to help me carry this unexpected burden. Outside, it was raining hard, and Abu Hazim—proud and compassionate—insisted on carrying the box all the way to our home in the Liftawi Building. We arrived home with our clothes dripping wet and started to guess at what this strange box might hold.

It was a tea set: forty-eight pieces of fine china cups and saucers and pots, all decorated with fine hand-drawings. Many times after this Abu Hazim visited us—we lived, after all, in the same building—and was offered tea in the usual glasses, until one day he happened to be there when we were visited by a relative of ours with her two young (and marriageable!) daughters. Suddenly the grand tea set appeared, and tea was offered around the drawing room. Here Abu Hazim refused it and said

"A glass is good enough for me!"

He carried on: "I carry it on my shoulder while God's rain is spilling down on us, and it never leaves its cupboard except to honor those who deserve it! I put my trust in God!"

From that day on the appearance of the tea set was a sure indicator of a guest's standing with my mother. With the repeated geographic scattering after the war my mother did not manage to keep her historic tea set.

Anis and Husam and I went off to the Palestinian Home Office building to put in an application for a 'reunion' identity card which would give me the right to citizenship—thirty years overdue.

Anis drove on to his job in the Ministry of Planning and International Cooperation in al-Ram, between Ramallah and Jerusalem, and left me with Husam, my guide to everywhere in Ramallah.

We went in to see the official in charge and I could not believe my eyes. It was Abu Saji, my good friend from the time of Beirut: open-faced and cool, generous and helpful and gallant. We embraced like two lost people who had given up hope and now found each other and found that they were well.

"I'm convinced they know their job now that I know they've chosen you to deal with people, Abu Saji."

I meant it. I gave him my documents. Tamim's birth certificate was necessary to get him a permit to enter Palestine. I did not have the certificate with me. I have to ask Radwa to send it.

A day or two and everything would be ready. We left the building.

Here my mother stood for as long as the sun was in the sky to get pieces of paper from the Israeli Military Governor. A new permit each time to visit her sons in Doha, Cairo, Beirut, Paris, or Budapest, or her brother in Kuwait, or to meet everyone in a hotel in Amman if everyone was able to get into Amman. Here she put in requests for 'reunion' and requests for permits for us to visit her that were always refused. This is the location for the daily exhaustion and bitterness for thousands of Palestinians throughout the years that Ramallah was occupied. Their problems are still there, complex and difficult to solve, but now a smile meets them in the place that—since 1967—witnessed the constant attempts to humiliate them.

True, life was not paradise before Israeli Occupation,

"We managed our affairs in our own way."

People say this, and then someone adds: "But the Occupation . . . "
And he falls silent.

Occupation prevents you from managing your affairs in your own way. It interferes in every aspect of life and of death; it interferes with longing and anger and desire and walking in the street. It interferes with going anywhere and coming back, with going to market, the emergency hospital, the beach, the bedroom, or a distant capital.

Everybody I spoke with here told me about their new favorite pastime of staying out late, an exaggerated staying-up in the houses of relatives and friends. But things here are temporary. The sense of security is temporary.

Israel closes down any area it chooses whenever it wants. It prevents people from entering or leaving until the reason for the closure is over. There are always 'reasons.' Barricades are set up on the roads between cities. I heard the word *'mahsum'* here for the first time. A *'mahsum'* is a barrier in Hebrew. The newborn feeling of freedom is temporary. Discussions continue (and will continue for a while) on the question of the 'resident' and the 'repatriated.' The system of relationships between the new Authority and the people is still to a large extent unwritten. The professors at Bir Zeit University tell me that until all the laws are in place to deal with all the human situations that take place within a framework of politics, economics, sociology, human rights, and individual rights, the arguments over the 'resident' and the 'repatriated' will continue.

I wanted my first meeting here to be with them. To pay my respects to them, and through them to this university. The Occupation punished it in every conceivable way and in return the university punished the Occupation in every way it could. I went to listen not to speak. To learn and remember and salute. I visited Bir Zeit University before I visited the village where I was born, Deir Ghassanah. I had met some of its students and teachers by chance in the various countries I lived in, but I had never stated my joy at their presence and their writings and their hopeful and positive example of continuous work under pressure and in cruel circumstances.

I have found the will and cultural commitment of Tania and Hanna Nasser remarkable and loved them for it. I met them often in the frequent times when the Occupation authorities closed down the university or during their holiday visits to Amman. I know about the problems the university faces and its financial difficulties, but I also hear that with the little aid it gets it puts up new classrooms and works hard to keep itself up to date.

On these beautiful hills I now see the old Bir Zeit School that has become a university of acknowledged academic status. The question of the 'resident' and the 'repatriated' was the one that involved the longest discussion in my introductory meeting with the faculty of Bir Zeit. Many sensitivities have to be taken into account to avoid mistakes in this area.

49

(In one of the ministries I saw that most of the directors were from the days of Beirut and Tunis. When a servant came in with the tea and coffee a director introduced him to me saying he was one of the "lions of the Intifada who gave the Occupation a hard time!")

On the tour of the university, with its colleges, its white stone buildings, and its classrooms, I found myself standing at the entrance of the Faculty of Science. There was a brass plaque commemorating the names of Palestinian businessmen in the Diaspora and some Arab businessmen from the Gulf who had contributed toward the Faculty building. I saw many names here, some of which I knew and many of which I did not. Among them was his name. How many of them can come here and see their names engraved on the brass squares that make up this plaque? How many, like Mounif, will never see it?

Three years ago, in our house in Amman, her young face under the headscarf was blank with sorrow. She wept as she embraced my mother, then sat among the mourners, a stranger in her silence. One of our relatives, sitting next to her, asked: "And how did you know the deceased, my daughter?"

"I didn't know him. I've never met him. I just knew his name. He sent my tuition fees to the university. I'm in the final year now and I read his obituary in this morning's paper and it had your address."

In the following days other students came to see us.

Every day I walked in the streets of Ramallah. I wanted to recapture the old images, the old rhythms.

Is it not odd that when we arrive at a new place living its new moment we start to look for our old things in it? Is there something

50

new for strangers? Or do they go around the world with baskets full of the stains of the past? The stains fall but the hand does not drop the basket.

I wondered if the people I passed on the street saw me as a stranger? Do their hurried eyes note the basket in my hand?

Every friend who heard of my arrival and came to see me took me to this place or that place in the city. I talked, I listened, I asked questions. Events, expeditions, phrases and who said them, and the order of things merged with each other in my mind. A feverish rhythm as though I wanted to take all of Ramallah back into my five senses in one go.

Now at the moment of writing about those days, I remember what I remember in no particular order. The order does not matter.

I prepare for the day of Deir Ghassanah. I prepare to go back to our first home there. I prepare to see Dar Ra'd.

3

DEIR GHASSANAH

Every house in Deir Ghassanah has a name. We never knew where the name of ours originated. It is probable that Ra'd was one of our ancestors because the other houses in the village were all named after people. You find Dar Salih, Dar al-Atrash, Dar 'Abd al-'Aziz, Dar al-Sayyid, and so on. I do not think that Dar Ra'd was an exception. We also do not know for sure how our family, which is supposed to be the largest family in rural Palestine, came by the name 'al-Barghouti.'

The ones who were proud of tradition used to tell us that the name derived from *al-birr*, 'piety,' and *al-ghawth*, 'succor.' And the ones who were proud of status and property said that our first grandfather was named 'Ghawth' and the vast lands that he and his sons came to own were then named *Barr Ghawth*, 'the lands of Ghawth.'

It seems to me a more reasonable etymology—although I admit it is less romantic and will not please or convince the 'notables' of the family—that the name derives simply from *al-barghout*, 'the flea.' Naming families after animals, birds, and insects is, after all, a common practice in old cultures: al-Far ('the rat'), al-Qitt ('the cat'), al-Gamal ('the camel'), al-Deeb ('the wolf'), al-Feel ('the elephant'), al-Asad ('the lion'), al-Nimr ('the tiger').

The late poet Abu Salma was having dinner with us once in Cairo in early 1977. Radwa was pregnant, and he was speaking about the birth of the first child in the family and what a unique and amazing experience it was; then he asked what we planned to name our child. I wanted to tell him about the names that Radwa and I had thought of but instead I said: "Suggest a name; an elegant, gentle, pleasant name. One for a girl and one for a boy, and I promise you we'll use it . . . ."

He thought and thought, then turned to me, and his eyes lit up with a mischievous smile as he said: "And where will I get you an elegant, gentle, pleasant name, Mourid, if you're going to follow it with 'al-Barghouti'?"

My fortunes with this name varied from one country to another, and they were not always negative. When I worked in the World Federation of Democratic Youth in Budapest and my job entailed a lot of traveling I was happy for my Spanish and Italian friends to call me 'Albargutito.' I used to say to myself 'Where are you, Abu Salma, to see the name you didn't like?' I even told some of my friends the story of the name—but only after I got to know them really well.

One summer when we held a conference for the Federation in Havana, Lilla, a Hungarian friend who spoke five languages and had spent her childhood in that city, took me to the Bodegito Café, a small, popular downtown café where they served *mojito*.

"What is *mojito*, Lilla?"

"It's Hemingway's favorite drink. He used to come and drink it here."

"And what's this chair hanging from the ceiling above our heads?"

She stood up, straightened the collar of her red shirt, and declaimed: "It is the chair that Hemingway used to sit on when he came to the Bodegito to drink *mojito* then along comes Albargutito, whom Lilla has invited out to have a nice time and he gives her a headache with all his questions!"

"Bravo!"

I applauded, then asked, "But in the end, isn't al-Barghouti a lovely name?"

"Don't be too happy," she said. "I asked Salim al-Tamimi what it meant and he said it wasn't much better than 'mosquito.'"

The Barghoutis did not allow their daughters to marry outside the family, which is why, as time went on, the family grew and grew. Only in 1963, the head of the family, Omar al-Salih al-Barghouti, gave his permission to a member of the family to allow his daughter to marry a suitor who was not a Barghouti. As for the young men, they had always been allowed to marry from other families but it was generally preferred that they marry a Barghouti girl.

You may find a Barghouti who is truly proud of this lineage of his and boasts of the rhetorical abilities of the family, its quickness of intellect and the sense of humor of most of its members. And you may find another, like Abu Rashad, who derives much enjoyment from telling of the hopelessness of the Barghoutis as landowners, and their lack of interest in the positions they held or the jobs they did. He says they were made for idle talk. Some of them owned entire villages, and lands that horses could gallop in but never thought, for example, of buying a car. Wealth did not change their lifestyle to go with the times. Then you find a third Barghouti who makes fun of both sides.

The Barghoutis live in seven neighboring hillside villages called the villages of Bani Zeid, and at their center is Deir Ghassanah.

We went to Dar Ra'd. A big house with a large, square courtyard, three sides of which are bordered by rooms; the fourth is part of the wall of the mosque in the village square. If you look down at the house from above you will see the cement domes that form the ceilings of the rooms surrounding the courtyard. A huge fig tree with a massive trunk and spreading branches dominated both house and courtyard. This tree fed our grandfathers and our fathers—there was not one person in the village who had not tasted its delicious fruit.

The gate of Dar Ra'd looks out over vast fields and olive groves that slope down gradually, their paths branching out and becoming more and more rough until they form the fertile valley watered by 'Ein al-Deir. 'Ein al-Deir is the source of water, of stories, and of the livelihood of the village.

I arrived at Deir Ghassanah in the company of Abu Hazim, Anis, Husam, Abu Ya'qub, and Wasim. At midday our cars came to a stop in front of the house. I crossed the threshold. I embraced my aunt, Umm Talal, and over her right shoulder I saw the fig tree—solid in my memory—absent from its place.

"Who cut down the fig tree, Aunt?"

Instead of the tree I saw a large cement block. The fig had been cut off at the point where its awesome trunk met the earth.

I greeted the neighbors and I recognized none of them. My aunt led me to the right, to the room that was ours in Dar Ra'd. The punishment was complete.

Does Dar Ra'd reject my story about Dar Ra'd?
Are we the same at parting and at meeting?
Are you you? Am I me?
Does the stranger return to where he was?
Is he himself returning to a place?

Our house!
And who will wipe the weariness off the other's brow?

Here my mother gave birth to me. Here in this room I was born, four years before the birth of the State of Israel.

The room is large and white, its high ceiling borne on columns rising out of its four corners to meet in the middle of a dome like those you find in old mosques and churches. Here we lived out our early days: my grandmother, Umm 'Ata, my father and mother, Mounif and Mourid and Majid and 'Alaa.

Someone has cut open a low door in the wall. It leads to my uncle Ibrahim's room and now both rooms together form the home of his widow Umm Talal. No one except her is left of the five families that lived in this house.

She has planted the whole courtyard with trees: grapefruit, honey apples, mandarins, apricots, plums; and some vegetables: lettuce, parsley, onions, garlic, mint. People will start calling us 'Dar al-Tur' ('House of the Bull') again, Aunt. (This was the title given to the people of Dar Ra'd and, again, nobody knows why. When we heard someone call us 'Dar al-Tur,' our parents said they had removed two of the dots on the first letter and we were now 'Dar al-Nur' ('House of Light'), but the title follows us to this day.)

"I've grown old and weak. People have emigrated and people have died. To whom should I feed the figs, my son? No one to pick the fruit and no one to eat. The figs stay on the tree till they dry and litter the whole yard. It wearied me and I cut it down."

My uncle's wife, Umm Talal, is all the residents of Dar Ra'd now. Alone. In the afternoons, her square courtyard becomes the meeting-place of forty-nine widows who are all that is left of her generation in Deir Ghassanah. Husbands, sons, and daughters have been distributed among graves and detention camps, jobs and parties and factions of the Resistance, the lists of martyrs, the universities, the sources of livelihood in countries near and far. From Calgary to Amman, from Sao Paolo to Jeddah, from Cairo to San Francisco, from Alaska to Siberia.

Some never leave their prayer mats and some never leave their whisky. Some study or teach in universities across the world and some went off with the fighters and never came back. Some have been absorbed by the professions: medicine, engineering, aviation, commerce. Some work in the Gulf countries and some in the United Nations. Some live on charity and some on petty fraud.

Everybody's income here is from the olive and its oil. People who can still work, work in the fields: men and women together as they have always done. But the work of sons or grandsons or husbands in the Gulf is the most important source of income. Expatriates send remittances to the village with travelers who hold identity cards or reunion permits and can come and go, or through banks in Ramallah and Amman. When thousands of Palestinians were thrown out of Kuwait after the Gulf War the economic situation of many families in the village was affected.

Rayyan ibn Ahmad, who owned a small bookshop in Kuwait that he had named Maktabat al-Rabi' ('Spring Bookshop') came back to Deir Ghassanah to breed sheep. Some returned to build a house on a piece of land they owned here and live on their savings. The people from the village who worked in Kuwait, in both the private and the public sector, had set up the 'Deir Ghassanah Fund' from which they helped those in most need. The Fund stopped when everyone had to leave.

Fatma bint Abu Seif, a most determined lady, decided at the age of seventy to restore the oil press that had not worked for years so that people could go back to pressing their own oil.

Abu Hazim gave his room in the upper floor of Dar Salih to Husam to set up a Computer Training Center. Husam bought three used computers and brought in an expert to teach the boys and girls in Deir Ghassanah. His first group will graduate in two weeks, he said, and he is getting ready to receive the second.

The people are forbidden to build or work on the outskirts of the village or in any areas that Israel considers part of its security arrangements.

After '67 my discovery that I had to buy olive oil was truly painful. From the day we knew anything we knew that olives and oil were there in our houses. Nobody from the village ever bought oil or olives. The village sells oil and olives to Ramallah, to Amman, to the Gulf. But for their own tables its people bring the olives in from the fields and the oil in from the press to the store-room and the barrels that are never empty from season to season.

For the Palestinian, olive oil is the gift of the traveler, the comfort of the bride, the reward of autumn, the boast of the storeroom, the wealth of the family across centuries.

In Cairo I would not let olive oil into my house because I refused to buy it by the kilogram. We weighed our oil in jars. It looked ridiculous in small green bottles like Coca-cola. But when absence grew long and going back to Deir Ghassanah became impossible, I exercised the first simple and serious humiliation when I put my hand in my pocket in a grocer's shop and bought my first kilogram of olive oil. It was as though I confronted myself, then, with the fact that Deir Ghassanah had become distant.

As for figs they vanished from my life in the years of the Diaspora until I saw them at a greengrocer's in Athens. I used to leave my hotel in the early morning to buy them for breakfast. I did not eat the hotel's breakfast once.

One summer in Vienna I saw them selling figs individually. I bought one fig for almost a dollar. I said to Radwa and Tamim that I had committed a crime against the fig tree of Dar Ra'd, and if my grandmother Umm 'Ata knew what I had paid for this one fig she would surely send me to Bethlehem.

"And why Bethlehem?" Radwa asked.

"Because that's where the lunatic asylum is!"

My first duty in Deir Ghassanah was to offer condolences to Umm 'Adli. 'Adli was a student in Deir Ghassanah school. The Intifada was at its peak. Israeli soldiers attacked the school to disperse the demonstration. 'Adli rushed to close the school gates, his arms wide open. One shot in the chest. One in the head. Blood on the iron gate, on the grass, on the shirts of the schoolmates who carried him back to his mother, who from that moment on was completely alone in this world.

Years ago she had lost father, mother, and husband. She lived for 'Adli, her only son, and 'Adli was martyred at the school gate. In Dar Salih, the biggest house in Deir Ghassanah, the house that was built four centuries ago and stands right next to Dar Ra'd, no other creature lives with Umm 'Adli. They have all gone.

Alone, with her face that carries the scar of an old burn, her peasant dress, her firm hands and green eyes, always sitting on the ground floor of the vast house. You look around and see the grass growing wild up the worn staircase (which leaves gaps as it winds up to the upper room), on the arches, even up the dark, time-stained interior walls. She gave me tea and a welcome and a motherly embrace. A defeated flash in the glance of the eye. She spoke of

Mounif and I spoke of 'Adli. We spoke a little and we were silent for a long time. Silence was what we could both manage.

I looked up at her father's upper room. *'Amm* Abu Hussein was the thinnest man in the village. He was illiterate but he was the best and quickest mathematician there. He was the accountant and the butcher—although he was neither by profession. But in the end somebody has to be good at maths, and somebody has to sell meat to the people.

He would ask all the men what they needed of a sheep he intended to slaughter the following day. One would want a shoulder, another some ribs, or a kilogram of cutlets, or a leg. He made sure he had sold every part of his sheep and memorized immediately what each man had ordered. Then and only then did he slaughter the sheep, distribute it in the village square, and collect his money. And if you were well known to him you could put your name down—temporarily—on his credit list.

Khala Umm Hussein bore him fourteen children, of whom four daughters remained. One of them is Hikmiya, Umm 'Adli. As for Abu Hussein, he died during my long stay in Budapest and I only heard the news years later.

We left Dar Salih and went to Dar Daoud to offer condolences for Lu'ay. Lu'ay met their bullets at the entrance to the village. We had recited the Fatiha for him as we passed the cement monument they set up where his blood fell. He threw a stone, they shot a bullet and left to the screams of the village. Neither Lu'ay nor 'Adli reached eighteen.

Now it is time for the meeting in the village square.

They expect me to do a poetry reading for the people of Deir Ghassanah. Today they are inaugurating the first 'cultural center' in the history of the village on the initiative of Anis and Husam, who have just come back from the United States and Amman respectively. They have invited the people of the neighboring villages of Bani Zeid.

I have completely forgotten what the road to Deir Ghassanah looks like. I no longer remember the names of the villages on both sides of the twenty-seven kilometers that separate it from Ramallah. Embarrassment taught me to lie. Each time Husam asked me about a house, a landmark, a road, an event, I quickly replied "I know." The truth is I did not know. I no longer knew.

How did I sing for my homeland when I did not know it? Should I be praised or blamed for my songs? Did I lie a little? A lot? Did I lie to myself? To others?

What love is it that does not know the beloved? And why were we not able to hold on to the song? Because the dust of fact is more powerful than the mirage of an anthem? Or because the myth had to descend from its lofty peaks to this real alleyway?

Israel succeeded in tearing away the sacred aspect of the Palestinian cause, turning it into what it is now—a series of 'procedures' and 'schedules' that are usually respected only by the weaker party in the conflict.

But what remains to the exile except this kind of absentee love? What remains except clinging on to the song, however ridiculous or costly that might be? And what about entire generations, born in exile, not knowing even the little that my generation knows of Palestine?

It is over. The long Occupation that created Israeli generations born in Israel and not knowing another 'homeland' created at the same time generations of Palestinians strange to Palestine; born in exile and knowing nothing of the homeland except stories and news. Generations who possess an intimate knowledge of the streets of their faraway exiles, but not of their own country. Generations that never planted or built or made their small human mistakes in their own country. Generations that never saw our grandmothers squatting in front of the ovens to present us with a loaf of bread to dip in olive oil, never saw the village preacher in his headdress and Azhari piety hiding in a cave to spy on the girls and the women of the village when they took off their clothes and bathed, naked, in the pool of 'Ein al-Deir. Yes, the preacher steals the clothes and hides them in the bramble tree so he may gaze long and hard at the tempting beauty of the women. Never in his life will he see temptation like this: not in the nightclubs of Europe, or his grandsons' louche parties at Lumumba University and various western capitals, or the sex shops in Pigalle and St. Denis, or even in the swimming-pools of Ras Beirut and Sidi Busa'id.

The Occupation has created generations without a place whose colors, smells, and sounds they can remember; a first place that belongs to them, that they can return to in their memories in their cobbled-together exiles. There is no childhood bed for them to remember, a bed on which they forgot a soft cloth doll, or whose white pillows—once the adults had gone out of an evening—were their weapons in a battle that had them shrieking with delight. This is it. The Occupation has created generations of us that have to adore an unknown beloved: distant, difficult, surrounded by guards, by walls, by nuclear missiles, by sheer terror.

The long Occupation has succeeded in changing us from children of Palestine to children of the idea of Palestine. I only started to believe in myself as a poet when I discovered how faded all abstracts and absolutes were. When I discovered the accuracy of the concrete detail and the truthfulness of the five senses, and the great gift, in particular, of sight. When I discovered the justice and genius of the language of the camera, which presents its view in an amazing whisper, however noisy this view was in fact or in history. Then I made the effort necessary to get rid of the poem that was an easy accompaniment to the anthem, to get rid of the badness of beginnings.

We used to crowd onto 'Abd al-Fattah's bus or Abu Nada's bus. It would be dawn and we would be accompanying a parent going on some errand to Ramallah. We would come back on the same bus, before sunset, to Deir Ghassanah.

I was entranced by the conductor, who climbed a ladder fixed to the back of the bus and energetically arranged the bags and cases on the roof then stood throughout the whole trip on the steps of the door near the driver. We called him *'al-kontrol'* and some called him *'al-kumsari'* in imitation and admiration of the Egyptian idiom.

Once I stood on the steps like him. The wind that came from the hills and the freshly-reaped fields swept straight into my lungs and made my white summer shirt swell and flap. From that moment on my dream was to become a bus conductor.

The joy of those few minutes on the steps of the bus was never repeated, but I envied the conductor for a long time. Sitting or standing in the crowded bus I could never fill my eyes enough with the fields of olives fleeting by, revealing small villages scattered over hill-tops of varying heights. I could not recall every detail of the road from Deir Ghassanah to Ramallah. All I could remember was that the traveler had to pass by both Bir Zeit and al-Nabi Saleh Wood.

Bir Zeit school became an important university; as for the small wood that was known for the density of its trees, Husam told me that it has been turned into a large Israeli settlement named Halmish. Israel took over the wood and large tracts of the lands surrounding it. It built houses and brought in settlers. The road leading to the wood—like all roads leading to settlements—is closed to Palestinians and for the use of the Israelis alone.

We passed the woods and entered the village of Beit Rima, the last place on the road before Deir Ghassanah. Husam stopped the car and said: "Get down and look at Deir Ghassanah from here. You can see it all at the top of the mountain. Look! As though it were on a postcard."

Villages are not defined by their houses but by their surroundings: fields, springs, caves, paths, mountains, and inherited stories changing from one generation to the next but somehow remaining as fixed as a book.

Deir Ghassanah has all these, but—oddly—is defined only by its houses. Stones that do not resemble the stones of the pyramids but manage to remind you of them, that do not resemble the stones of the walls of Jerusalem but are chiseled from the same quarries. Thick, dark, dull stones. Houses that have the air of fortresses without being fortresses, that hint at romance but are far from romantic. Practical houses inhabited by rich and by poor, by the clever and the idiotic, the illiterate and the educated. Houses that are hundreds of years old. Their entrances are vast arches, their roofs are domed. (Muhammad al-Abrash used to tether his camel under the gateway arch of Dar Salih and the large beast would look puny.)

Houses on the hilltop. Houses on my mind. I entered them all in my childhood. I remember the cement domes, the thick walls with moss growing in their cracks. I remember how close together they were and I remember every detail of the arches traced by their roofs on the high blue of summer.

"Mourid! I burned it down! But it came back and grew again. Would you believe it?"

Husam pointed at a palm tree growing out of the wall of his second-story room in Dar Salih. A palm tree spilling her young fronds into the air over the fields.

"A palm tree, man! Would you believe it?"

Plants that grow in the stone and live for hundreds of years. Decaying houses, but their closeness to each other, seen from here, gives an impression of solidity and strength. We came closer.

We passed the school. The first thing you see when you enter Deir Ghassanah. It was built in the 1920s, and every child in all the villages of Bani Zeid studied in it. They walked tens of kilometers to get to it. They rode donkeys. Teachers and students crossed the valleys and the floods of winter.

Nobody in the whole of Europe would have believed me if I had told them that the teachers, parents, cleaners, headmaster, and hundreds of children at my school—I the individual, the stranger who leaned toward silence and solitude—all belonged to the same family and carried the name 'Barghouti'!

Here I was given religious instruction by Ustaz 'Abd al-Mu'ti al-Salih al-Barghouti. In primary school we did not know that he had been a communist when Lenin was alive, and that he had been jailed for this in the late twenties and early thirties. This same Mr. 'Abd al-Mu'ti was a relative of ours and the father of Fadwa, Abu Hazim's wife, and her brother, Husam.

This, then, is Deir Ghassanah, which is recorded in my birth certificate and which fills the gap for 'place of birth' on every one of the passports I have carried through my many places of exile. And next to it always the 'date of birth': 8 July 1944.

Deir Ghassanah, which is recorded in the Foreign Student

65

Archives of Cairo University, and in the Foreign Prisoners' Bureau and the Khalifa Department of Deportations, recorded in foreign languages on the entry visas to faraway capitals. The name I pronounced every time I was asked "And where are you from, brother?" Most were not content with my answer but had to hear the word 'Ramallah'; the name of a place they already knew.

Now Deir Ghassanah is about to leave its place on the documents and become real. Real in its dark colors, its dirt roads, its narrow lanes, its cemetery surrounded by thorny cactus plants procreating constantly even so close to death and the dead. Its minaretless mosque, its guest house in the middle of the village square, its arches and domes, and the smell of the cattle that carry the plowmen to the fields and the wells. Umm 'Ata carrying her water-jar on her head from 'Ein al-Deir to our thirst and our cooking and our washing and the ewers that we were taught to pour the water from over the hands of our guests after they had finished eating the food prepared in our ovens.

Deir Ghassanah is no longer an idea or an entry in a file. She comes out of abstraction and looks at me as I cross her. Soon, when the engine of Anis's car comes to a stop, she will know me. She is about to open the huge parentheses in which thirty years of life will be placed; my displacement will be contained in parenthesis.

But among all the children playing in the streets there were none who knew me.

I had no right to feel that slight tremor. But I felt it. I wanted someone to know me. Even that old man walking slowly and thoughtfully along the street did not know me. And I did not know him, and I did not ask. How stupid in your own birthplace to ask a tourist's questions: who's this and what's that?

The closer we drew to the village square the clearer I saw the traces of departure, of desertion. Slow progress comes in its own time; in the absence of its people, electricity came to Deir Ghassanah, television aerials rose on some roofs, the fresh black of asphalt lit up one or two streets.

We draw closer. The deserted houses tell their stories in eloquent silence. I should have imagined the decay in the arches and the gateways, the roofs, the thresholds, and the steps. In fact I expected to see this desolation that I see now in Deir Ghassanah when I saw the sad changes in Ramallah. If the Occupation had so handicapped the city it was natural that it should do the same to the village, completing the village's historic despair of gaining civic elements to enrich it and help it to grow.

I noticed a tall minaret at the end of the village and asked if the people had built a minaret for their mosque. Husam said they had built a new mosque. The red slogans of Hamas are still legible on the walls of Dar Salih and the mosque and Dar Ra'd. In the square I saw that a small section of the school—ruined many years ago—had been efficiently and beautifully restored. I had heard that a leftist Italian organization had donated some funds to build a nursery school here. Some of the owners of the land were wary; they were afraid of the project and suspicious of its aims. They tried to stop it. They leveled various accusations at those who showed enthusiasm for it.

Ownership in the village is divided between tens of heirs scattered across the globe. Some of them do not even know they have inherited land in Deir Ghassanah. It is practically impossible to get all the heirs to take a unified position on any piece of land or house or olive field. But they calmed down when they saw the restoration or pictures of the new nursery.

This, then, is the village square. This is the guesthouse of Deir Ghassanah, where the men meet every night to talk or condole or celebrate a wedding or receive a guest from a neighboring village or a far country. At once I smelled the scent of dark coffee and cardamom coming from the far end of the guesthouse wall where Yusuf al-Jabin pounded the coffee in the wooden mortar with a dancing rhythm. The square, the guesthouse, in front of me now and available to my five senses. Stone, not images—my eyes see it for the first time in thirty years.

They stood up in front of me in their bodies, their clothes, their white headdresses, their faces. They stood up as though they had not died. They stepped out of a poem into which I had written them in my exile. My father. *'Ammi* Ibrahim. *Khali* Abu Fakhri. Abu 'Ouda. Abu Talib. Abu Jawdat. Abu Bashir. Abu Zuhair. Abu 'Izzat. Abu Muti'. Abu al-Mu'tadil. Abu Rasim. Abu Seif. Abu Adel. Abu Hussein. They were resurrected on their mat of colored straw whose pattern—forget what I would all these years—would never escape my memory.

An appetite for the men who built in the guesthouse
A place of generosity,
A home for sly jokes,
A home to mock the powerful,
A home for the night as long as an argument
And the news of every country,
As though the mat underneath them
Were a United Nations!

But they were not resurrected. Not the village headman nor the plowman. Neither the generous nor the miserly. Not those who loved us nor those who hated us. Neither the good nor the cruel. They grew old in death and their places grew old too.

Since I left the naivetés of childhood behind me I no longer wish to retrieve the dead so that they come back as I have known them in my past or theirs. I do not want to recapture Deir Ghassanah as it was or my childhood in it as it was. I know the meaning of time passing. But this is no metaphysical matter. I know what it means for cities and villages to be under occupation.

In the last few days Ramallah told me a great deal about what the Occupation had done to it. And now the village tells the same story. Even at the moment of the return after a long absence, the moment that tempts the most hard-headed to lose themselves in romantic mists, I found no tear to shed over the past of Deir Ghassanah and no yearning to recreate the village as it was in my childhood. But questions about the crime of occupation made me think about the extent of the 'handicapping' practiced by the Israelis.

I have always believed that it is in the interests of an occupation, any occupation, that the homeland should be transformed in the memory of its people into a bouquet of 'symbols.' Merely symbols. They will not allow us to develop our village so that it shares features with the city, or to move with our city into a contemporary space. Let us be frank: when we lived in the village did we not long for the city? Did we not long to leave small, limited, simple Deir Ghassanah for Ramallah, Jerusalem, and Nablus? Did we not wish that those cities would become like Cairo, Damascus, Baghdad, and Beirut? The longing always for the new age.

The Occupation forced us to remain with the old. That is its crime. It did not deprive us of the clay ovens of yesterday, but of the mystery of what we would invent tomorrow. I did not come here to reclaim al-Abrash's camel. I used to long for the past in Deir Ghassanah as a child longs for precious, lost things. But when I saw that the past was still there, squatting in the sunshine in the village square, like a dog forgotten by its owners—or like a toy dog—I wanted to take hold of it, to kick it forward, to its coming days, to a better future, to tell it: "Run."

4

THE VILLAGE SQUARE

I did not turn my back on romance because of a fashion in art; it is life itself that has no task but to destroy the romanticism of humans. Life pushes us toward the dust of reality.

Buildings are not the only things destroyed by time. The imagination of the poet is preordained for destruction. Suddenly my imagination collapses like a building. When I saw them whole as though they had not died, they died forever. There was nothing in the guesthouse except their absence. My tremor is meaningless now.

I wondered if this was comparable to what happened to me when I was permitted to return to Egypt and live there after a seventeen-year prohibition: I could not fulfill the needs of romanticism (expected by lovers of melodrama) in this return to a city in which I had studied and worked and lived for many years.

Radwa told me that the years of petitioning had paid off and my name had been removed from the prohibited lists at Cairo airport. I could return and live with my family with no conditions. I was in Amman and getting ready to travel to Casablanca as a guest of the Arab Writers' Union to take part in the Arab Poetry Festival that was normally held alongside the General Writers' Conference. Radwa too was invited—with other Egyptian intellectuals—to the same conference.

She left Cairo two days before I left Amman and we met in a hotel in Casablanca. I entered the lobby. Radwa detached herself from a group of friends and headed for me with her arms open wide in the midst of the comments of the writers sitting in the lobby drinking Moroccan tea.

My suitcase this time was large. It carried the clothes of someone taking up permanent residence rather than visiting for two weeks. We telephoned Tamim every day and he started waiting for his father's return home to settle.

I do not return to Radwa. I return *with* her. As though she had taken me by the hand to bring me back to the house they tore me from, and from her and from Tamim, one ugly, distant, autumn day.

Outside the airport, Tamim had lost all patience, even though everybody had prepared themselves for a long wait.

Cairo airport is, in any case, a difficult one for the impatient traveler. Everything happens with a slowness caused by people who think they are doing their job well. It is a point of view.

We went into the house by night. (A strange thing: all returns happen at night—and weddings and worry and pleasure and arrests and deaths and the greatest joys. Night is a thesis of contraries!)

We did not sleep at all. The three of us chattered our separated lives in houses that came together to become one house.

As the days passed I began to understand. You do not rejoice immediately when life presses a button that turns the wheel of events in your favor. You do not arrive unchanged at the moment of joy dreamt of for so long across the years. The years are on your shoulders. They do their slow work without ringing any bells for you.

I come back after I have placed the body of Mounif in the darkness from which no one ever returns. After the fear of the future has returned to haunt my mother. Tamim prepares for the final school certificate exams, the nightmare of every pupil in Egypt. When they came for me, I was fetching—from under the balcony—his washed nappy, ripped by the November wind from the clothesline. He was five months old, sucking with his lips in the happiness of infants wrapped in woolen shawls watching the nipple in the clear-skinned breast approach their clear-skinned faces. Now he is a man who shaves his beard and moustache. Three years ago we bought him a shaving kit and clothes only one size smaller than my own.

I had to divide my memory between the absurd past, the concrete present taking shape with Tamim and Radwa in our house, and the future that could not be determined by our decisions alone. And dividing the memory between an old weariness and a new-found comfort was impossible. Memory is not a geometric shape drawn with instruments, mathematical decisions and a calculator, an area of glorious joy next to an area of pain. The scales of need were unbalanced despite us all. The three of us needed the same nearness at the same time to the same degree. Sensations of a new beginning and of the resumption of a broken past jostled with each other. The clarity of the 'return' to the house was crowded by the uncertainty of the common future of the family and those close to it in faraway places.

We had had to bear the 'clarity of displacement' and now we had to bear the 'uncertainty of return' as well. And we did. We realized—and it was a discovery—that the one who returns comes back with burdens on his shoulders that a sensitive person can see as he sees a porter bent double in the fog of a port.

What is needed here is slowness. The vibrations of the past will take their time until they calm down and find a form in which to rest. This needs the slowness of a magician. A precious slowness, allowing feelings of comfort and calm to work their way gently within us. These feelings do not form at once or suddenly. Slowness teaches us how to accept the new; to regard it as natural and the way things have always been. We have to live the new intensely and slowly.

We learn this together. And our house learns to see us once again together. It gets used to our repeated mornings with crumpled night-clothes and half-closed eyes looking for the slippers and discovering that one of us has to go out now at once to buy some coffee because we ran out last night and we did not notice. Radwa waited seventeen years for me to come back to our house, and when I came back I brought all those seventeen years with me. And there were seventeen years with her too.

From the time I was deported, every time I was permitted to come back to Cairo I would spend as long as possible inside the house. I would look at the house: look at the brown sofa next to the bookshelves. At the curtains with their abstract pattern, at the small desk by the window, at the rough drafts and the missing sentences. Each temporary return completed the other half of a sentence. For all displacement is a semi-sentence, a semi-everything.

They snatch you from your place suddenly, in a second. But you return very slowly. You watch yourself returning in silence. Always in silence. Your times in the faraway places watch too; they are curious: what will the stranger do with the reclaimed place and what will the place do with the returned stranger?

As for the relationship with the city, that is a different story. In Cairo the world had sorted itself out without me in my long absence. Friendships had gone their own, improvised way. Some landmarks remained in place, but not in exactly the same place. A coffee-shop had closed down. Friends had adopted a new one. Groups had formed and so had enmities. Positions, ambitions, and loyalties had been realigned. People's daily schedules had been designed and it was difficult for a newcomer to find a place in them. The friends of the past were living lives dictated by necessities and choices about which I knew nothing. The fortunes of those who start out with you on the same road turn in contradictory ways; one becomes a man of influence, another loses his talent and other talents are invented for him, one becomes an editor-in-chief, another works abroad, a third has forgotten you, and the fourth you have forgotten.

In 1973 Radwa told me she was going to study for her PhD at the University of Massachusetts. I liked the idea. She went, and I remained in our home in Mohandiseen for almost two years. The house was always crowded with friends; friends who had already established a presence on the cultural scene or who were still feeling their way into film, or theater, or music, but primarily poetry. My first collection of poems had appeared at the beginning of 1972 and I was in touch with an entire generation of intellectuals. When I returned to Cairo that community had scattered. Death or different destinies meant that I no longer met up with that early seventies group except by accident.

When you meet friends from the past you find that everything is different. One day I joked to a Hungarian friend who used to help with the printing of the Federation magazine in Budapest: "All my girlfriends have left me, Zsuzsa. What should I do to get them back?"

I will always remember her reply: "We have a proverb in Hungary, it says: a dish of cabbages can be heated when it grows cold, but it will never taste the same."

The taste of those early days has been lost. I do not particularly like cabbages, nor do I like talking about human relationships in terms of food, but folk consciousness everywhere is brilliant at summarizing the human condition.

The impossibility of feeling absolute joy in the thing found after losing it was exemplified in my return to Cairo. I was surprised that my imagination carried on working—even though I was acutely conscious that I walked on the land that had occupied my imagination for many years.

What is it that was lost in this that I have found? A specific look of the sidewalks I trod? A rhythm? A type of sunrise and sunset? Footsteps I waited to hear—and heard—one desolate night? Wisps of fog that formed themselves into a shape that pleased me one early morning? A row of trees down the center of some road? It is always the same problem: the problem of stitching two times together. It cannot be done. Time is not a length of calico. Time is a mist that never stops moving.

Say you are romantic. Time will coldly discipline you. Time makes us reel with realism.

This is the grave of *Khali* Abu Fakhri.

Here the 'king' lies under the dust. A giant with a gentle voice. In his features a mixture of de Gaulle and Antony Quinn. Ever since I knew him he smoked a pipe; he stuffed it with the worst kinds of tobacco, which he called *heisha*. He was the only one among the villagers who smoked a pipe. He could be proud of a new garment for only one day, because the next day it would have a charred hole from the pipe that never left the corner of his mouth. He surprised me once by saying: "Your uncle went to Port Said, boy."

"And why did you go to Port Said?"

He answered as though I had asked the most stupid question: "So that I would go to Port Said!"

One night he set off with his gun for al-Bitara, his olive grove outside Deir Ghassanah, because he had heard there were thieves there stripping the olives. He came back with a bandaged index finger because he had shot himself.

He lived on his income from the olive seasons. Most of the year there was not a piaster in his pocket because of his generosity with the little he had. He was more comfortable with his friends than he was with *Khalti* Umm Fakhri, who learned her excessive caution from his excessive generosity. Once when she was away from the house he invited all the neighboring children and handed out his grandchildren's old clothes that she insisted on keeping forever. Then he was afraid of her anger. He brought a rope and tied himself to a chair and waited. When she returned he told her that thieves had tied him up and stolen her grandchildren's clothes. But she was a smart woman and did not believe him, and the story turned into a family anecdote.

Khalti Umm Fakhri was a remarkably small woman. You noticed it particularly when she walked next to him. When they crossed the bridge together coming back from Amman the Israeli soldier finished Abu Fakhri's papers first. When he did not move and the soldier tried to move him along, he said he would wait for his wife, pointing at Umm Fakhri. The Israeli looked at the giant Abu Fakhri, then at his wife. He asked in broken Arabic: "How many year you with madame?"

"Fifty years, *khawaja*."

The Israeli smiled: "Donkey!"

"You see, Umm Fakhri—he knows me!"

When I learned to write, I wrote his letters for him. I never loved any of our relatives as much as I loved him. He died while I was in Budapest, and his children split up and went to Saudi Arabia, Jordan, Austria, the Emirates, and Syria. Not one remains in his house.

I mourned him and his son. Fakhri was like his father: generous, spontaneous, and merry. His jokes and quips: his personal dictionary ensured that anyone who talked to him did not stop laughing. He visited me in Budapest with his wife, Su'ad, and their youngest daughter, Molly. A few years later he died in Saudi Arabia and was buried there.

Here is the shop of Yusuf al-Jabin, a peasant, a barber, and a great dancer of the *dabka*. The wall it shared with the guesthouse has collapsed and its roof has fallen in. Its entrance is blocked with rubble.

We come closer.

The almond field owned by Umm Nazmi, who could not bear to see one of us children get away with a single almond from the huge trees, has become a cemetery. I beg her forgiveness for the image of her that crept into my *Qasidat al-Shahawat* ('Poem of Appetites'):

An appetite for the thievery of the child within us,
Slipping through the miserliness of the old woman whose face
Was like biscuit dampened with water,
To steal the almonds from her field.
Our pleasure is that she should not see us.
And more pleasure, should she see us in running away.
And more pleasure yet
If her cane catches one of us
And whips him.

After lunch Anis suggests we rest for a while in his house. We entered the large, many-roomed house through the ruined gateway, the debris like a small hill impeding the entrance.

Shahima and Zaghlula are the only women here. They are both over seventy. They have never married. They are both short, but Zaghlula is a little shorter than Shahima. On their faces the wrinkles are almost identical. They live in this vast ruin entirely alone and neither of them will speak to the other: for years now they have been in a permanent state of feud and mutual boycott. When the gateway collapsed, Abu Hazim joked to our relatives in Amman that the two women entered and left the house by helicopter!

When Anis came back from America he fixed up one room so he could live in it. The heat and exhaustion had got to me. I took off my shirt and lay bare-chested on the cool floor. I fell asleep with my arms stretched out as though on a crucifix. I woke up to the noise of everyone getting ready to go to the square for the poetry reading. What should I read?

I ask myself the same question before each reading, without exception. And this reading is an exception in itself. I gave in to my habit of deferring the choice to the last minute: when I face the audience from the stage.

When I write poems, the audience is not defined. But they become defined when I am asked to read. The specific receiver. This alone makes the choice easier. I did not write for 'them' specifically but I shall read for 'them' specifically. I have always followed this system, and the spark between me and the audience has always caught fire; I felt it and so did they.

I remember particular readings, in Cairo, in Amman, in Tunis, and in Morocco. But tonight is puzzling. Do they actually want to listen to poetry? Or are they greeting my safe return and doing what should be done? I left the choice to the last minute and mounted the small platform outside the guesthouse.

These, then, are their faces. The old men who escaped death and the young ones who managed to stay. Behind them sit the grandmothers and aunts and the forty-nine widows. As for the children, they did not stop running about, surprised to see their village square turned into a theater. Husam and Anis say some of the young people in the village staged a play on the roof of the mosque in this square in 1949.

Before I stepped up onto the platform I went around the audience and shook hands with them one by one: men, women, and children. Some remembered me. Some remembered Mounif. All of them remembered my father. They called him *al-Hanun* ('the tender-hearted'). Anis and Husam, with their customary sensitive courtesy, introduced people whose names they felt I may have forgotten. "This is al-'Afu, Abu al-'Afu's son," Husam said. I shook his hand warmly. A young man, tall, blond-haired, and handsome like his father. I came to your father's wedding, al-'Afu, in this square an age ago.

"So you are the son of Abu al-'Afu."

In an instant the scene from the past forms itself in front of me: Mounir Abu Zaki, a slim young man in a thin white shirt, leads the line of *dabka* dancers at the wedding of his brother Fakhri (who will later become Abu al-'Afu). The girls of the village have turned the roof of the mosque into a terrace from which they sing and clap and trill out their joy-cries. The dancers are desperate to stay in a position from which they can see the girls. But Abu Zaki keeps their backs to the mosque, and he alone can look up at the terrace. He is the leader and they have to keep their eyes on his feet and his steps.

I was a child when I saw that wedding in this square where I stand now to read in the first poetry evening in the history of this village. I do not know how or why Abu Zaki's dance stayed in my memory all these long years when all the dancers have scattered. Abu Zaki went to Sharjah and Abu al-'Afu died. And events threw me from Deir Ghassanah to Ramallah to Cairo, to Kuwait, Beirut, and Budapest. And in Budapest I put the whole scene into a poem, "A Wink."

I stood in the square in Deir Ghassanah. Behind me the wall of the guesthouse. To my left Dar Salih. To my right the wall of the mosque. In front of me the wall of our house, Dar Ra'd.

Mounif's body fills the place. Not a ghost or a memory. He himself with his height, his glasses, his fair face, and his smooth hair, in this ruined square for which he had commissioned studies and plans for restoration. He wanted to turn it into an open-air theater, into artists' workshops. He wanted to build a nursery school and an agricultural college here. He had plans to bring the arches and the domes and the gateways back to their former glory.

I was with him once in the French village of Ivoire, and I was taken with its age, its flowers, its rich cultural life. He said: "Deir Ghassanah, if we look after it, can be like Ivoire and better."

Yes. Everything around me, everything within me dictated that I should begin with my elegy for him. I wanted to bring him back here, carried on my language. I wanted him with me.

A motherly man
Whose motherliness shaded his mother
To see her smile,
Who feared that in the wool of her coat
There might be one sad thread.
Who dared to bend his cypress height?
Who dared to send this tremor
Into the air around his shoulders?
Who dared to kill beauty's last cry for help?

I read 'Bab al-'Amud' and other short poems. My audience was moved. They laughed. They were saddened. My sense of them was powerful and all-enveloping.

The slogans of the Intifada, although its actions had ceased because of Oslo, covered the walls of the mosque and of Dar Ra'd, covered everything that could be written on by chalk or paint. Most of them the slogans of Hamas. The mind moved toward the catastrophes of politics and politicians—but this is a poetry reading. Let the thoughts form. Form and settle in the heart with the rest of the bitter rubble.

These people need no more bitterness. Let there be in your poems an indication—however faint—that, in the end, life goes on with the living. I reminded the people of the wedding of Abu al-'Afu. I dedicated the poem to Mounir Abu Zaki (wherever he may be) and read.

A wink of her eye at the wedding
And the boy went mad!
As though parents and the night
And the shoulders of the young men taking refuge from sorrow
* in the dabka*
And the aunts and the headman
Had all become nothing.
He alone is the leader of the dance,
In his waving handkerchief the whole night shakes,
And the girl who singled him out for that pure light,
She alone is the village.
He stretched his right hand as far as it would go.
He shook out the handkerchief twice and thrice,
He let the djinn ride on his shoulders then threw them off and
* bowed,*

*He let the djinn ride on his knee then threw them off and
    straightened.*
A foot he planted in the earth for a second,
The other thrown up like a hammer then settled like a stake.
If he almost fell at the clap of a hand
He was held up by the pull of the flute.
He catches the dark like desire from the towers of night,
Exact as the light of her eyes.
The chest and its hair sweat with his swaying right and left,
And the sweat of the back falls perpendicular.
The heart's shyness hid all that was in it,
And the white shirt wet from the shoulders to the leather belt
Showed a spine where you could count the discs.
Another wink even if I die here!
Another wink even if I wait forever!

There are moments when poetry is subjected to a sudden test,
when it is read to an audience that is not particularly concerned with
literature or poetry. I had this experience twice in the last few years.
Hayfa al-Najjar, the headmistress of the National Girls' School in
Amman, invited me to give a poetry reading for the students, girls
between ten and seventeen years old (naturally enough, at that age
they do not have a history of reading or listening to poetry). This is
the second time.

I recite in front of 'my uncles,' as I called them when I took hold
of the microphone, in front of the headman, the plowman, the shep-
herd, the mothers, the grandmothers, the educated, the illiterate, and
even the children, all gathered in this village square in which a poet
had never stood before.

In the school in Amman and here in the guesthouse of Deir

Ghassanah some of my anxiety disappeared, and so did my doubts about the relationship between 'ordinary' people and what we write. At the end of the evening I said to Husam: "There is no neutral audience, my friend." There is no completely innocent audience. Each person has his own experience of life, however simple.

For the first time in my life I read my poems in front of row upon row of villagers in their traditional dress, among them the eight-year-old and the eighty-year-old; most of them had never entered a theater or owned one volume of verse. 'Abd al-Wahhab, the village madman, fell in love with the daughter of the headman in the 1950s and used to write her the most touching love poems. We children (to his great surprise) used to tremble with fright whenever we came across him in the village or in 'Ein al-Deir because he was mad. But he was not mad at all. He was described as mad because he wrote poetry and also because he wanted—he who had nothing—to marry the daughter of the headman!

The reading was over and the discussion with the people of the village began. Questions about displacement, estrangement, returning, and the political situation. But the question I still remember came from a lady in the back row. She said: "What is the most beautiful thing you saw since you returned to the homeland?" I replied quickly and truthfully: "Your faces." I climbed down from the platform, my feelings a mixture of happiness and mysterious sorrow, and I found myself surrounded by children. They held out their pencils, their school copybooks, pages torn from their school copybooks, for me to sign. They pushed forward, their eyes full of that enchanting childish mixture of shyness and mischief.

It might have been a moment of pure happiness, apart from that voice that scolded me, that said: "Wait a minute!" A cruel and hurtful thought: What does Deir Ghassanah know of you, Mourid?

What do your people know of you now? What do they know of the
things that you have been through, the things that have shaped you,
your acquaintances, your choices, the good and the bad in you
throughout the thirty years that you have lived far from them? What
do they know of your language? Your language that in some ways
is similar to theirs and in some ways different, the language of your
mind, of your speech, of your silence and isolation, your language
in conflict and in contentment? They have not watched your hair
turn gray. They do not know your friends or your habits, and if they
did, would they like them? Your position on the concept of family,
on women, on sex, literature, art, politics? They do not know the
bad traits you rid yourself of and the others you acquired since you
left them. They think you were not that upset about the cutting
down of the fig tree. They do not know Radwa or Tamim. They do
not know all that has happened to you in their (your?) absence. You
are no longer the child in first-year primary they used to see a long
time ago, walking across this square on his way to the multiplication tables or the dictation lesson. Do many people remember? In
any case, they are not required to remember. You too do not know
the times they have been through. Their features that you remember are constant and altered at the same time. Have they not
changed also? Umm Talal, unusually, speaks about politics. They
tell me that many of the young people of the village are enthusias-
tic supporters of Hamas. Umm Talal is more attached to the fig tree
than I am. Cutting it down must have been necessary at a particular
moment that I do not recognize because I was there and she was
here. It is that simple. Perhaps if it was I who had carried on living
here I would have knocked down or built, or planted or cut down
trees with my own hands. Who knows? They lived their time here
and I lived my time there. Can the two times be patched together?

And how? They have to be. These boys and girls, if they had seen me with their fathers and their uncles in their homes every evening for thirty years, would they have asked for my autograph in their books as a strange poet?

Abu Hazim suggested that we get back to Ramallah before dark. Since my arrival the Government of Israel had decided to close down the West Bank because of the General Election and their fear of the operations of Hamas. The tension was tangible.

The road between Deir Ghassanah and Ramallah was surrounded by settlements. At night their lights are a clear indication of their size. The largest is the settlement of Beit Il on the outskirts of Ramallah. That is the border of Area A, which is an area of Palestinian authority. The road itself falls under the category of Area B, which is under joint Palestinian/Israeli supervision. This means that the real authority is in the hands of the Israeli soldier. I was told that this is the case for all roads between the Palestinian villages and cities.

It was not possible to go to 'Ein al-Deir, the kingdom of *'Ammi* Abu Muti', who spent eighty years sowing and watering and cutting canals and dividing the slope of the hill into graded ledges, permitting the water to settle and preventing the soil from sliding away. From the beginning of the century until his death a few years ago he had been harvesting the olives in sacks and carrying them to Abu Seif's press. At 'Ein al-Deir he grew every plant that would grow in the climate of this land: honey-apples, figs of every kind (*khodari, sawadi, bayadi, khurtmani, safari, zuraki* and *hamadi*), oranges, lemons, grapefruit, pomegranates, quince, mulberries, onions, garlic, parsley, lettuce, peppers of every kind and color,

sweet yams, cauliflower, cabbage, *mulukhiya*, and spinach. He did
not respect the wild herbs that grew without his personal care such
as mallow, sage, chamomile, *murrar* and *khurfeish,* even though he
used to try to teach me their strange names and stranger properties
in the treatment of diseases. He was a master of water. He was
able—an illiterate man who had never left the village—to irrigate
the entire mountain or the entire valley with the least amount of
water, not wasting a drop, as though he were the most resourceful
agricultural engineer. He was a man of small size whom his son,
Muti', described one day as having "stayed the size of an orange"
despite all the food that he planted and cared for. "'Ein al-Deir is
ruined, my son," said Umm Talal. "It's overrun with brambles. The
jackals wander in it freely. Go see with your own eyes." I did not
go. I do not want to go.

My head on the pillow in Abu Hazim's house. Another home for the
traveler, another pillow for the head. My relationship with place is
in truth a relationship with time. I move in patches of time, some I
have lost and some I possess for a while and then I lose because I
am always without a place. I try to regain a personal time that has
passed. Nothing that is absent ever comes back complete. Nothing
is recaptured as it was. 'Ein al-Deir is not a place, it is a time.
Evidence of the last rain that we can see on our shoes even though
our eyes tell us it has dried. The thorns of the brambles trained our
hands and our sides to bleed early when we were children returning
home at sunset to our mothers. Do I want to scramble through
brambles now? No, what I want is the time of scrambling. 'Ein al-
Deir is specifically the time of Mourid as a child, and *'Ammi*
Ibrahim, a peasant and a hunter. His traps drew the birds from four
green hills to flutter in the end between his exultant fingers in the

game of sky and earth. He used to talk to me a lot about the stupidity of birds who would see the grain of wheat but not the trap. And when he was satisfied that I had seen their stupidity with my ear and my eye he would add the sentence that I did not understand when I was five or six years old: "People, young man, are like birds. Many of them see the bait and don't see the trap."

Dar Ra'd is not a place, it too is a time. A time of waking up with early prayers to taste the figs picked by the light of the dawn. Figs washed by the dew and pecked by the energetic birds—nobody can tell when fruit is ripe as well as a bird can; birds are not really that stupid. It is the time of the jar of olive oil that has arrived this minute from Abu Seif's press to the hot bread in my hand before I set off for school. It is that sudden (innocent?) contact with the breast of the neighbor's daughter while we play, the contact that means you can never go back to your first innocence. This is it. You now know, even if only in the rush of play, the feel of the breast of a female. He who knows is not innocent.

The places we desire are only times but conflict is over place. The whole story is about place. They prevent you from owning it and so they take from your life what they take. When a journalist asked me what longing meant for me I said something close to this. It is the breaking of will. It has nothing to do with the mellowness of memory and remembering.

Because of the many places that the circumstances of the Diaspora made us live in, and because we so often had to leave them, our places lost their meaning and their concreteness. As though the stranger prefers the fragile relationship and gets edgy if he feels it becoming strong. The vagrant holds on to nothing. The one whose will is broken lives in his own internal rhythm. Places for him are means of transport to other places, to other conditions, as though they were wine or shoes. Life does not allow us to consider repeated uprootings as tragic for there is an aspect to them that reminds us of farce, and it will not allow us to get used to them as repeated jokes because there is always a tragic side to them. Life teaches us to be content with the only fate proposed to us. It tames us. It teaches us to get used to things. The person on a swing gets used to moving in two opposing directions; the swing of life carries its rider no further than its two extremes, farce and tragedy. The world swings on, a light mist hiding the two horizons. In Cairo, on the morning of that dark historic *'Id*, there were six plainclothes policemen. When Tamim's nappy, still damp, fell off the line and I went out to fetch it I saw them: six agents in a car belonging to the State Security Service. I said to Radwa: "They have arrived."

5

LIVING IN TIME

They took me to the Passport Department in the Tahrir Building. In the evening they took me home to collect a suitcase and the price of a plane ticket. On the road to the Deportation Center at Khalifa, to wait for their final decision, I looked my last on the streets of Cairo. The swing of tragedy and farce moves with me, with every bump of the jeep and every flicker of the form of the coming days. The six men appointed one of them to watch me pack my bag; the five others sat in front of our television and—without asking permission—started watching the live transmission of the president's speech in the Knesset. What will the days bring for this five-month-old child, for Radwa and me, for us? It was only on the plane, when I was in my seat, that they took the handcuffs from my wrists. I said lightly to my neighbor: "Farewell, Africa." I had done nothing to oppose Sadat's visit to Israel. It was a preventative deportation, the result of a false accusation put together, as we found out after several years, by a colleague in the Union of Palestinian Writers. As you see, life will not be simplified.

From Baghdad to Beirut to Budapest to Amman to Cairo again. It was impossible to hold on to a particular location. If my will clashed with the will of the owner of a place, it was always my will that was exposed to breaking. I do not live in a place. I live in a time, in the components of my psyche, in a sensitivity special to me.

I am a child of mountains and stability. Since the Jews of the twentieth century remembered their Holy Book I have been afflicted by a Bedouin traveling, and I am not a Bedouin. I have never been able to collect my own library. I have moved between houses and furnished apartments, and become used to the passing and the temporary. I have tamed myself to the feeling that the coffeepot is not mine. My coffee cups belong to the owner or are left behind by the previous tenant. Even breaking a cup acquires another meaning. A coincidence of estate agents alone is what chooses the color of my bed linen, the color of my curtains, the color of my cooking pots. I do not choose. Chance chooses. Several times I have given up all the geraniums that I grew on the changing balconies. I choose my ceramic pots for my house plants—my yucca, my syngonium, my dracaena, my schefflera, my bear's foot, my fern—I arrange them and look after them and wash them, leaf by leaf in beer. I dip a piece of cotton wool in the beer (which is better and cheaper than chemicals), I hold the leaf in my left palm and wipe its surface gently with my right until it gives off that wonderful shine that brings to my mind the final bar of a symphony. I move from leaf to leaf and from one plant to the other with the same care. I turn on the music for them and let it play constantly while I am out of the house. I start my day by touching their leaves and branches and checking the dampness of the soil. I watch the degrees by which they turn toward the sunshine coming in through the window or the balcony. I move them from their places to let them turn their

91

shaded side to the sunlight. Sometimes I support some of their branches with special sticks, and sometimes I tie them to transparent threads that prefigure the way the plant would want to grow. I give them light and air and friendship and then I leave. I always leave. I give up the possessions of displacement in a routine way without emotion. Except when I am distributing my house plants among friends in the country that leaves me or that I leave.

But in airports and at borders and in the temporary rooms of hotels I forget everything that lies behind and ask about the shape of the days to come. The shape of time, not the shape of place. Exiles have sudden journeys, hotels weave their way into our lives. Theoretically I should have hated hotel life since it emphasizes transience. Perhaps I should have hated it but practically it became clear to me that that was not exactly the case. I felt comfort in hotels. They taught me not to hold on to a place, to accept the idea of leaving. Gradually, through the many short journeys that I had to take, I started to like the idea of a hotel. Hotels absolve you from immortalizing the moment but at the same time provide a theater for short acts and surprises and a widening of the monotonous horizons of life. In a hotel you are exposed to unique marvels. It gives you something of the taste of temporary permanencies. You collect messages from friends every time you come back from a short walk. It constructs for you, immediately, a small community of friends in the new city you have just arrived at. Something like a family of those who care for you for a few days or for a few hours in the day. In the hotel there is no neighbor to watch what you do all the time. There are no traps of social obligation. It is the place where you can glory in laziness. You leave it and come back to it at improvised hours. It is the temptation of a day wide open. In a hotel you are not responsible for the plants or for changing the water of the vase that is replicated in every room. This is a vase it does not pain you to leave. You have no books to worry about giving to friends and neighbors before your enforced departure, a departure planned by others. There is no cruelty in leaving the paintings hanging on the walls of your room. They are not yours and mostly they are ugly.

I contemplated the guesthouse on whose platform I stood. This is my first place. The faces of its men and their voices come back to me. Or is it my imagination borrowing them from their long death? They appear and disappear in front of me with their real characteristics and those that had been stuck on to them by the tongues and stories that the Barghoutis are supposed to be masters of. The late poet 'Abd al-Rahim 'Omar says that in Ramallah there are Muslims, Christians, and Barghoutis! The older folk tell the tales of the guesthouse to their children, generation after generation. Their tales are clothed in exaggerations and additions, depending on the sense of humor of the teller. Some came to me from my father and some from Abu Hazim, but most are stored in their original form in the memories of Abu Kifah and al-Mu'tadel. Abu Kifah's main targets are an uncle of his called Samih and another uncle, Majid. As for al-Mu'tadel, because of his intelligence, he was allowed to sit with the adults from an early age, and later he spent all his vacations from his work in Saudi Arabia at the guesthouse.

Here is Abu 'Ouda, sitting at the farthest corner of the mat (the distance from the center of the mat depends on the wealth of the sitter). Suddenly one summer evening Abu 'Ouda says: "Do you know how people distinguish between a stupid man and a clever one?"

"How, Abu Tunub?" (It is said that he was given this name because of his early pressure on his father to let him get married; a 'tunub' for them is a long penis.)

"A stupid man has a broad beard."

Nobody commented, but the headman, sitting in the center of the guesthouse, lifted his right hand slowly to feel his beard, and all the men burst out laughing!

Once he said to them: "Your village, you people of Deir Ghassanah, is a hypocrite's village. If Abu 'Ouda speaks pearls you say you didn't hear, and if the headman farts you say the scent of musk!"

And here is 'Bismarck,' the father of al-Mu'tadel, who manipulates and fixes the affairs of the village in a mysterious way. His nickname reflects not just his machinations but the attitude of the villagers who gave it to him. The nicknames the village gave to people quickly replaced their real names. One of the cleverest similes I heard during this visit concerned two friends who were always together. It was said that they were like Kleenex; if you pulled out one tissue the other appeared immediately. Here is Abu Zuheir, the most cunning man in Deir Ghassanah, who got his son Zuheir married to a girl and then married her sister himself when he was seventy and fathered the martyr 'Adli.

And here is Abu Seif, awesome and huge, the biggest landowner in this village and its surroundings. The Israelis built a settlement on his land in the village of Mlabbis and named it Btah Tikfa. He is the owner of the olive press in Deir Ghassanah. He married a girl from Damascus sixty years younger than himself and she bore him a son a few months before he died.

Here is Abu Jawdat, old, generous, always sleepy. And Abu Talab, who lent money with interest. And Abu Muti', in his everlasting silence, as though this transient life did not concern him. Although it did concern him. I asked his wife, Hakima, for news of one of our relatives in Kuwait. She said, in a tone full of pride:

"Praise be to God—his position is high, high. May God be pleased with him. Refrigerators, washing machines, air-conditioning units, video recorders, radios, cars—with one stroke of the screwdriver he fixes them all."

And here is *Khali* Abu Fakhri, telling of his days in the Turkish Army and in the Red Belt Brigade, and his traveling with Umm Fakhri because of his job. He used to go to the butcher in Ramallah and breakfast in the early morning on kebab and liver. He had the most beautiful smile despite his gold teeth, because his smile was formed essentially in his eyes.

These are the images in the memory. But they are not the only images. The camera set up from this angle brings out their beautiful side. When it is moved to another angle it would bring out less attractive features in them and in their time that has passed but has not passed. From among these men who are the ornaments of the guesthouse a group rose one winter morning to lead two small girls in fourth-year primary across the square and into the mosque and asked them to recite a chapter from the Quran. The children hesitated and stammered.

"What do they teach you then at school?"

"Dictation and mathematics and drawing and songs."

They took them back to our house and the house of the headman, for one of them was the daughter of the headman, and the other was Sakina Mahmoud 'Ali al-Barghouti, who would later become my mother. Abu Muti', Abu al-Mu'tadel, Abu Zuheir, and others announced a decision that my mother will never forget. She tells us the story in its most minute detail and she is angry and defeated as though she lives the moment again every time she tells it.

The girls' school in Deir Ghassanah only went up to fourth-year primary. This was not because it was difficult to add new classes to

95

the school, nor was it because of the scarcity of women teachers in Palestine. It was because the girls, after fourth-year primary became, in the view of the village, women who should be 'stored' in their homes to wait for marriage, and they should stop going out, even if only to school.

That year, the headmaster of the Friends' School for Girls in Ramallah came to the village and decided to give a scholarship to the two top girls in fourth-year primary to carry on studying for their Secondary School Certificate at his school in Ramallah. He said they would live as boarders in the residence for girl students and the school would give them every care and all the expenses that they needed. The men in the guest house went crazy.

"This is a missionary school and will ruin the girls' minds."

"The teachers, even in the village, don't ask the girls to learn the Quran by heart, so what do you think if they take them to Ramallah?"

The two children in their enthusiasm to continue their education drove the guesthouse mad. Bismarck came up with the idea of examining the two girls in the Quran.

"Listen, Umm 'Ata, your daughter is forbidden to go to Ramallah—understood? Take her and store her at home. Your daughter has reached puberty and she is forbidden to carry on playing in the square—understood?"

They did not intervene to prevent the daughter of the headman from continuing her education. As for my mother, another child went in her stead—a child whose father was not bothered about the opposition of the village. Her name was Fawziya. Adiba, the daughter of the headman, continued doing well and later obtained the Secondary School Certificate from the Friends' School. She became a teacher, then the head of a distinguished school in Palestine. But

Fawziya was unhappy with her new situation and returned to the village after a while. The child Sakina, the daughter of Mahmoud 'Ali al-Barghouti, was the only one who was deprived of her one chance of an education. Because she was a fatherless child.

Her father had died when she was two years old, and left her mother (my grandmother) pregnant with a child who only saw the light after his father's death. Her dead husband's people wanted to throw her out of the house. Why should they look after a widow who had no money but was burdened with a child and was carrying another?

"I beg you, let me stay in the house a few months, just until I give birth. Perhaps God will be good to me and the child in my belly will be a boy."

"Agreed, but you must know that if you have another girl you take yourself and the two girls and you go back to your people's home."

The baby was a boy. She called him 'Atallah. He became *Khali* 'Ata and the reason they allowed my grandmother to remain in Dar Ra'd, the home of her departed husband. She was not yet twenty and looking after two fatherless children alone.

Those who wanted the young widow pounced to ask for her hand. Abu 'Ouda said to her: "A camel in place of a camel."

Abu Mahmoud asked for her and insisted, and others asked and she refused them all. The village started to treat her badly. They could make her life miserable but they were not able to break her resolve to devote her life to looking after her two fatherless children, *Khali* 'Ata and Sakina, my mother.

Sitti Umm 'Ata lived nearly ninety years, and toward the end of her life she lost her sight. She died in 1987. She was pleasant and light-hearted but had her own way in everything she said. One day she was sitting in her usual corner in the house and Umm Talal was in the house looking after her while my mother was away for medical treatment. Suddenly *Sitti* said to Umm Talal: "Open the veranda for me, Ratiba."

"Why, Umm 'Ata?"

"I want to throw myself out and be rid of you."

When I lived with the family of *Khali* 'Ata in Kuwait she was with us. I used to stand behind her while she prayed, without her seeing me, and when she turned her face at the end of prayer to say *"al-salamu alaykum,"* I would surprise her with a kiss on her cheek. She would start and stretch out her hand to hit me, saying, with a hint at my relationship with Radwa and my intention to marry her: "Go kiss your Egyptian girlfriends."

Sitti never married after her husband. She died while I was in Budapest.

On her last day
Death sat in her arms.
She was tender to him and pampered him
And told him a story,
And they fell asleep together.

As usual, I was far away and did not take part in the final farewell.

This too is an image of the men of the guesthouse. It is our life and their lives, with the good and the bad. We have a right to live it and not defend it. Yes, this life that is sometimes cruel and is certainly not ideal. This is our image too: *Sitti,* who moved from Dar 'Abd al-'Aziz to marry in Dar Ra'd and be treated like a stranger, as a refugee from another people, another planet, even though the distance between the two houses was a row of almond trees not longer than a hundred meters.

This is our image too: *Sitti*, whose baby boy was the reason she was given the right to remain in her husband's home, lavished all her care upon him at the expense of her girl child. But in any case she was not mistress of her own life and certainly was too weak to insist on her daughter's right to an education and to travel to Ramallah.

When she was over fifty, my mother joined classes for adult education to satisfy her thirst for knowledge, and she taught us her biggest lesson, which was that the most important value in life is knowledge and that it deserves every sacrifice. Fadwa Tuqan visited us once in Amman and made us a present of her book *A Mountain Journey, a Difficult Journey*. My mother was the first to read the book. When she had finished it she said to me: "My voyage was more difficult. Fadwa never saw what I saw."

In my university years I felt that I was getting an education simply for her sake; to see her happy. I would be ashamed of failure, as that would make her sad. This was made more intense by the feeling that she had concentrated all the meanings of her life in us, her four children. As for everyone else, she loved them as much as they loved us. Her children were the world and this was a shortcoming that she saw as a positive thing. She could not bear for one of us to be away from her, and the sad thing is that we all went away and stayed away for a long time. As for the best of us, the most precious of us, he left never to come back, and she had to bear it. In her mind she would arrange and organize a comfortable world, a world in which everything went the way she wanted it to, as though she wanted to be on her own planet.

She wants to go to a planet away from the earth
Where the paths are crowded with people running to their rooms
And where the beds in the morning are chaos
And the pillows wake up crumpled,
Their cotton stuffing dipping in the middle.
She wants the washing lines full and much, much rice to cook for
    lunch
And a large, large kettle boiling on the fire in the afternoon
And the table for everyone in the evening, its tablecloth dripping
    with the sesame of chatter.
She wants the smell of garlic at noon to gather the absent ones
And is surprised that the mother's stew is weaker than the power
    of governments and that her pastry in the evening
Dries on a sheet untouched by any hand.
Can the earth contain
The cruelty of a mother making her coffee alone
On a Diaspora morning?
She wants to go to a planet away from the earth
Where all directions lead to the harbor of the bosom,
The gulf of two arms
That receive and know no farewells.
She wants airplanes to come back only.
Airports to be for those returning,
The planes to land and never leave again.

Love for her is work. Attention. That she should be attentive toward those whom she loves, should tire herself out for them. Should do—with her own hands and her own effort—everything she can possibly do; from managing the house to managing life itself. From making pickles in season to sewing and embroidery and using leftovers to make new and dazzling objects. She once turned herself into a designer and carpenter to refashion and upholster an old set of drawing-room chairs and sofas. She supervised the building of a house with rooms for all her sons and their wives and children. She went over the blueprints with the architect, who told me that she had objected to the location of the kitchen in the drawings: "The kitchen here will be dark. I want you to put it facing East not West."

He said: "She was right. We changed it."

Every time I see those women who make a profession out of belonging to political parties coming up with their well-rehearsed revolutionary phrases, my faith in the revolution of actual work carried out by our mothers deepens: a revolution realized every day, without fuss and without theorizing.

When I read the biography of Giacometti I was completely taken with what Eve Bonnefoy had to say about his mother; Anita Giacometti was a woman of powerful and fascinating personality:

> She was the center, the vigilant and silent guardian who seemed to keep a tradition alive by her presence alone, the guardian of the family, the deep-rooted source of their strength, the one person who knew things, who could state facts and recognize values, who could tell what one ought to want and what one must decide, and she was also the person who unhesitatingly expressed opinions which were often orders, whether about daily duties or the great crises of life.

My mother has several of these characteristics, as well as a kind of settled beauty, comfortable with its years, and a spontaneous and calm femininity slightly hidden—even from herself. But her desire to throw her protection over everyone reflects her wish to keep us all children for as long as possible. Her obstinacy aroused our admiration sometimes, but sometimes made us wonder. My father handed the reins of the household to her; to her he left all crucial decisions. It was enough for him to agree. He was fifteen years her senior; a man of so calm a character that it was difficult for him to keep up with her fiery rhythms and effervescent initiatives. His goodness led him to treat her always with pleasant affirmation. He believed that what was right was what she decided. He was justly called 'the tender-hearted,' for he was gentle and—with his almost mystic patience—was content with life as it was.

As for my mother, there were no limits to her ambition. What she could not achieve she expected her sons to gain. And if not her sons, then her grandsons. She is utterly certain that "if one wills, one can." She is still—at over seventy-five—a free spirit, rebelling against every restrictive social convention. She does not stop working in the house and in its little garden: she plants and waters and sets up small walls. With her own hands she moves the stones that she needs to build a small terrace here or to map out a flowerbed there. And she has green fingers; anything she plants in the garden or in a pot lives and grows and blossoms. When she talks about her trees she says: "This tree is ignorant," meaning it's too young to bear fruit.

Or she says: "An idiot tree," when it's fully grown but shows no signs of fruit. When a guest visits she gives him a cutting of basil, vine leaves, or gardenia, and when it wilts in his home he brings it back for her to look after and 'treat,' and sure enough it flourishes again.

Sitti Umm 'Ata had one sister, whom *Khali* Abu Fakhri married. We grew up loving him because he stood by her and gave my mother and her brother all the tenderness of a father without a father's wish for control. *Sitti* took her two children and moved in with her sister Umm Fakhri, and it was Abu Fakhri who looked after both families and carried the responsibility for everyone in good times and bad.

They woke up in front of me, these people of Deir Ghassanah, with their wonderful and wicked stories. They were the children of their characters and their time.

I used to see them in the circle of the *dabka*, their arms linked over each other's shoulders, waving their white *kufiyas* high in the air of the village square. Some were cruel and some were tender, some were generous and some were miserly, yet they all danced to the husky song of the flute, happy to be marrying off a young man or to receive a bride into the village, alike and parallel like the teeth of a comb.

We had to wait a long time for life to teach us—on our long journey toward wisdom and sorrow—that even the teeth of a comb are not actually alike.

6

UNCLE DADDY

In the morning I went with Abu Hazem to look at the house of *Khali* Abu Fakhri.

"What do you want?" a young man shouted from the balcony of a neighboring building. Abu Hazem answered: "This is the home of our relatives. We just wanted to look at it."

"But we have an official rental contract," the young man said.

The three arched stories, the white stone, the small lemon orchard next to the house, its pretty iron gate covered with rust. It is clear that no hand has done anything to it since 1967.

"Come inside," the young man said. We thanked him and left the place. That he should suspect our intentions is understandable. Everybody here fears for what they have. Many people have registered their possessions in the names of their relatives so that the Occupation cannot confiscate those possessions as belonging to absentees. This is how the Palestinian lands and homes, whose owners work in the Diaspora, were saved. This is how the olive groves were maintained and how the land was looked after and plowed and turned and combed and watered. If it had not been for the mutual trust between those who were there and those who were absent, Israel would have confiscated everything.

But it must be said that some people behaved as though the return of the Diaspora Palestinians were a miracle that would never happen. Some absent owners stopped following the affairs of their belongings and some of the resident caretakers stopped paying the dues on the property left in their care. There are dazzling stories of the faithfulness and commitment of the 'caretakers' to the rights of the absent owners; rights not registered in contracts or through powers of attorney. But there were also stories about residents who actually took possession of properties that they were holding in trust and refused to return them to their original owners. (Life, as you see, will not be simplified.) A few of the 'caretakers' are afraid that the returning owners will ask for what was theirs before the Occupation. It could be olives or homes, or flats that were let at very low rents, simply to keep someone in them as a kind of protection.

Abu Basil, who came with others to visit me, told me that he had registered his home and his land in the name of his sister while he was working in Saudi Arabia. When he managed to obtain the reunion permit and came back to Deir Ghassanah he found that his sister had registered the house and the land in the names of her sons. He had nowhere to live. Nobody will go to the courts of the Occupation, whatever the reason and however big the loss. But these days you can see members of a family holding things against each other.

Since some people started returning to Palestine immediately after the Oslo Agreement, we have been hearing of cases similar to that of Abu Basil. My friends and I agreed that it was tempting to write a play—a comedy—about the changing fate of people we knew as a result of these new circumstances. Each one of us added a sentence to what had gone before: "So-and-so returns to Deir

Ghassanah and asks his cousin to give back the olive field he was looking after in return for an agreed wage."

"But the cousin who has tasted ownership for thirty years and enjoyed it says to him calmly: 'You left nothing with me. Pave the sea or hit your head against the wall if you wish.'"

"A heart attack ensues immediately."

"The wife sees her husband dead—she goes mad."

"The children see their mother mad for the death of their father so they kill their cousin."

"The old uncle sees this Shakespearean massacre in Deir Ghassanah and commits suicide with a large can of gasoline that he pours over his own head."

"The gasoline spreads to the corner of the house, then the other houses, then the guesthouse, then the guests and the nearby fields. Deir Ghassanah burns."

"Just like *Paris is Burning.*"

"You have a wide imagination," Abu 'Awad said as we played cards on the night when snow closed down Amman. Then he cried: "Trump!"

He asked me: "Is it true that you used to play whist in Beirut in the middle of the Civil War?"

"Yes, it's true," I said.

"Aren't you ashamed of yourselves? Trump!"

It is true. We had nothing to do on the nights of bombing and barricades and slaughter except play cards. I would say to al-Derhalli as I scooped up the ace of spades he held so dear: "Good old *Sitti* Umm 'Ata. Perhaps even now she's looking up at the sky and praying: 'God give Mourid ibn Sakina victory and protect him from bastards wherever he is, for the sake of the Prophet.'"

And Derhalli would say: "Perhaps my mother is saying 'I wonder if Derhalli's warm? I wonder how he's living there? Does he have warm covers in this cold? May God protect him and save him. God be with the young ones, all of them. Turn on the radio here, Fatima, so we can hear the news of the young ones . . . ' Trump!"

Prolonged wars generate boredom. One evening I had a competition with Rasmi Abu 'Ali to think of all the folk synonyms in the different Palestinian dialects for the verb 'to slap.' There was a power cut, naturally, and each one of us was in his bed talking to the other without seeing him. We left no word but we remembered it. He says goodnight and we are silent for a few seconds, and then one of us remembers a fresh word and throws the quilt off his face with a victorious gesture, crying out "*Sannuh kaff,*" for example. And the whole competition would begin again. That night we got through *jabaduh, qahaduh, raza'uh, lahuh, shaffuh, haffuh, sanaduh, laffuh, lattuh, rannuh, safaquh, nadafuh, zahuh, habaduh, raqa'uh, lakhkhuh, faq'uh, lahafuh, tajjuh, maza'uh, shamatuh, nawluh.*

A huge rat shared the flat with me, and all the wars of extermination that I fought against him were no use. The flat had no heat and no carpets. Those who were talented in arranging their personal affairs always lived in splendid flats, with elevators and emergency generators, but tension was common to everybody. My youngest brother 'Alaa lived in the student lodgings of the American University. He was in his final year in the Faculty of Engineering and it was difficult to see him every day. If he visited me I worried about his return to Hamra, and if I visited him I hated to worry him about my return to Fakihani. Fahim, the son of *Khali* 'Ata, was hit in the head by shrapnel in Shayyah after I left Beirut.

He died a few days later. He was twenty-two. Afterward I learned how they broke the news to my uncle. He was in Kuwait when 'Alaa called him from Beirut. 'Alaa's idea was to attempt to get my uncle to accept the news gradually: "*Khali*, I'm calling to tell you about Fahim. He was hit by a stray bullet yesterday but the doctors say that God willing he will recover well."

My uncle's calm response was: "Where are you going to bury him?"

His two sisters, Ilham and Najwa, his brother Mahmoud, and my brother 'Alaa put him in a coffin and took him by plane to Kuwait, where they buried him in the Salibkhat cemetery.

Amherst, Massachusetts, USA. We were getting ready for a short trip at the invitation of Professor Sidney Kaplan (who insisted I call him Sid). He had invited us to dinner in celebration of Radwa being awarded her PhD under his supervision. The telephone in our apartment rang. Mounif's voice was abrupt: "Fahim was martyred today in Beirut."

Mounif is calling me in *America* from *Qatar* about Fahim's martyrdom in *Beirut* and burial in *Kuwait*, and about the necessity of informing *Sitti* Umm 'Ata in *Deir Ghassanah* and his maternal grandmother in *Nablus* and my mother in *Jordan*. Radwa and I are confirming our tickets to return to *Cairo* via *Rome*. Radwa decided that it was better for us to be with Kaplan and his wife and Michael Thellwell, instead of spending the night alone on this continent. Everybody was very nice to us. Emma had clearly gone to a lot of trouble over the dinner. The atmosphere was warm and intimate and conversation flowed. Radwa was right. With friends the burden of sorrow is lighter. I crept into the bathroom in

Kaplan's house and made every effort possible to stifle the sound that accompanied the vomiting.

And not everything was sad that evening or in the time of our stay in America. There we got to know some African and African-American writers and found in them a remarkable closeness to our atmospheres and the cultural and political problems that troubled us Arabs. This was the healthy, vigorous attitude of opposition to the American establishment. In Thellwell's house I had the best and strangest breakfast I have ever had. He invited Radwa and me one morning and the breakfast that he prepared himself—for he was a skilful cook—consisted of strips of fried mango, strips of grilled fish, cheese, and coffee. At that table we met Stokely Carmichael, and Radwa introduced me to Chinua Achebe and his wife. The poet Julius Lester translated with Radwa a long poem of mine called "Sa'id the Villager and the Beauty of the Spring." Radwa showed the translation to Kaplan and over dinner in his house he said it was "Whitmanesque." His wife said that this was the highest praise Sid could give for he adored Walt Whitman. I swelled with pride of course, but now with my present sensibility I see that the poem did not deserve such high praise.

That night in Abu Hazim's house I lay in bed and tried to count the number of houses I had lived in. I counted up to thirty.

On the veranda, Fadwa told me that Umm Khalil would come to visit me after work, and that Saji would come with her. Abu Hazim added that Bashir al-Barghouti telephoned this morning and invited everybody to dinner at his house. Fadwa's daughter, Sawsan, phoned from Amman and her sister, Leyla, from America. The telephone, now that the era of letters is over, is the sacred tie between Palestinians. On the West Bank and Gaza the telephone has developed into the mobile carried in the pockets of the representatives of the newborn Authority in a way that antagonizes ordinary citizens. They are antagonized even though they know that normal land lines are not available on the West Bank and Gaza and that there is a kind of necessity for the mobile. But other things contribute to their feelings: the kind of houses that are bought by the ministers, the undersecretaries, and the directors, or even those that they rent at high prices; the luxurious cars they ride in. The marks of personal power do not fit with the absence of their national power or with the power of Palestinians in general according to the strange arrangements of Oslo.

When people are content they will look at the practical side of a commodity's function. A car for some people denotes personal status, for others it is a pair of shoes to cross distances and move us from place to place. The latest manifestation of power and status for the Arab parvenu is the mobile phone. In Beirut, glory was in the buttock over which hung the gun from the belt of the adolescents of the Civil War, the journalist, the writer, the civil servant, the party member.

As for the car, it seems that as a status symbol it is here to stay, particularly as the optional extras develop year by year. Can the person whose car has air bags be equal to the person whose car has not? Is the man who has a driver equal to the poor wretch who has to drive himself to work?

All these associations that are beside the point (what is the point?) took place in the silent fragment of a second, in preparation perhaps for the Moroccan proverb I repeated to Abu Hazim and Fadwa on the veranda: "God protect us from the deprived if he gets a taste."

In the afternoon, Umm Khalil and Saji came. Saji and I studied together in Cairo but I remember meeting him there only very rarely, though we were in the same university, the same college, and in the Department of English Literature. He devoted most of his time to political work. Saji was made for politics. He was passionate about the Student Union and the secret party life that formed a focal point for many students in Cairo then. I did not go along with them.

I gave political activity no importance at all in my Cairo days. I did not know what the objectives were. I was completely happy and absorbed studying the subjects on the syllabus. There I learned about Chekhov and T. S. Eliot and Shakespeare and Brecht and Greek civilization and the European Renaissance and the New Criticism. I turned my back for the first time on traditional *('amudi)* poetry and started trying to write free verse *(qasidat al-taf'ila)*.

Mounif was working in Qatar and used to send me the equivalent of 18 Egyptian pounds a month. I paid 9 pounds for rent and on the remaining 9 pounds I lived and went to the opera every Saturday night to listen to the Cairo Symphony Orchestra (the ticket cost 19 piasters) and managed to go to the National Theater and others. In his first letter after I was admitted to university, Mounif wrote that he would set a condition that I should always exchange the dollars that he sent me in official Egyptian banks: "If I learn one day that you exchanged your money on the black market you will return to Ramallah immediately. You are at the beginning of your youth and if you start your life crooked you will never be straight."

When Mounif wrote me these words he was just twenty-two years old.

In my years at university I used to talk to my colleagues about my 'big brother' and tell them some of his news that came to me in regular letters. Once I showed Radwa his photograph and she said in

111

surprise: "But this is a boy! You say, 'my big brother, my big brother.' I thought he was an old man. He looks younger than you!"

Years later, when we married and she met him, she was confirmed in her feeling for his sweetness and endearing youthfulness. Mounif was three years older than me. He was born in Jericho in 1941 and I was born in Deir Ghassanah in 1944. 'My big brother' was a phrase that reflected his role, his maturity, and his responsibility, all of which were greater than his age.

I have to confess to my lack of interest in politics at that period—I, a Palestinian, the son of the disaster of 1948. I went once or twice to political events to which I was invited in the headquarters of the General Union of Palestine Students in Gawad Husni Street in Cairo. But I felt that I did not belong at all in that movement and that I was no good for it and it was no good for me.

Years later, the development of events, the defeat, and the appearance of the various factions of the Resistance made me realize that the years in which I studied in Cairo from 1963 to 1967 were the years of the secret formation of the armed Palestinian organizations—Fatah, the Movement of Arab Nationalists *(Harakat al-Qawmiyin al-'Arab),* and others—and that this formation was taking place within the framework of the Student Union. Those students who used to invite me so cautiously to their political activities were carrying out large projects. They must have thought me either extremely naive or a coward. If I had understood the true nature of what they were doing, would I have fulfilled their expectations and joined them? I do not know.

One of the things my mother could be blamed for is that she taught us an excessive caution about putting ourselves in any kind of danger. None of us to this day can ride a bicycle: she feared that one of us would fall off and break an arm or a leg. Later, I would look at those colleagues and relatives who became freedom fighters as though they had been created to be heroes while I had not. They must be a better kind of human being.

Saji continued his political work. He became a member of the political bureau of the Democratic Front. His mother, Umm Khalil, became famous in the world when she put herself forward as a candidate for the presidency of the Palestinian Authority: the only rival to President 'Arafat.

We agreed that in the morning I would visit the headquarters of the Society for the Support of the Family, which she headed. And I agreed with Saji and Walid that we would go out the same evening for a night out in Ramallah.

In the evening we went to dinner at Bashir al-Barghouti's.

"Oslo can lead us to independence or it can lead us to Hell. We have to do better at everything if we want to avoid the second possibility," Bashir says.

He understands the new situation. He lives in the homeland, edits *al-Tali'a* magazine, and is the secretary of the Palestinian People's Party. A few days before he had been appointed Minister for Industry in the new-born Palestinian Authority. Bashir has a serene, contemplative face. He usually does not speak much, but on an evening like this we had to run through the various events and incidents and jokes from Deir Ghassanah. With us that evening were his wife, their son Nabil, and her sister Noha (my colleague from the days of school in Ramallah) and her sons, and Anis and Husam and Abu Hazim. I hadn't seen Noha since '67 but I heard a lot about her voluntary activities from various European women who had worked with her for stretches of time in the homeland.

Next morning Maliha al-Nabulsiya came to visit with two of her eight sons. She used to be our neighbor in the building of *Hajja* Umm Isma'il. I said to her: "You've been relieved of the Israelis dragging the children to the Detention Centers, *Hajja* Maliha"

"Thanks be to God, my son. I had enough. They let one go and locked two away. And poor Maliha has to go and ask which detention center or which town they've put them in, and are visits allowed or not. The rheumatism—may evil stay far from you!—has exhausted me, but between you and me, in the days of the Intifada the world was better. What do you think?"

I agree the world was better.

"Do you think they will really pull out? That Netanyahu, you can't believe a word he says. He is evil, you don't know him."

When I asked her if Peres was better than him, she waved her hand: "The two are worse than each other." Then added: "They're all bastards."

Maliha has eight children whose father was martyred in the second year of the Intifada,

"We thank God he was martyred at the beginning. We were passionate, our morale was in the sky, above the wind. I bore his death, I said: 'What has happened to him has happened to others.' If he had died toward the end I would have burst. They ruined it at the end, my son. I swear by God they messed with it and dirtied it so that people would be happy when it stopped. What do you think?"

When I mentioned that the Palestine Liberation Organization gives financial assistance to the families of the martyred she said quickly: "The organization isn't regular. One month they pay and ten they don't. They say the donor countries don't give them the funds. God be with everybody. They used to give 50 dollars a month when they had money, but we are managing, praise be to God."

It is very embarrassing when the home of your host is filled with your guests. Abu Hazim said: "It is like honey on my heart," and Fadwa seconded him. But sometimes friends came to see me close to midnight and I was embarrassed that my hosts had to stay up later than they were used to. I had to find an occasion to broach the subject of a hotel without hurting Abu Hazim's feelings. The occasion came when I wanted to call a taxi to go to Ramallah Hotel to meet Mahmoud Darwish, who had arrived the previous day from Amman. I said: "If you could find me a room in the same hotel, Abu Hazim, that would be better for me and for my erratic program that can't be organized in a way comfortable to everybody." Abu Hazim and Fadwa's reaction meant that I had to apologize to them for even thinking about a hotel.

I took a taxi, met Mahmoud, and we talked about many things, among them the possibility of issuing *al-Karmel* magazine once again from Ramallah. Then I went to see Umm Khalil at the Society for the Support of the Family.

I went round the different sections of the Society: sewing, embroidery, crafts, fruit preparation, packaging, and wrapping. Here daughters and sons of martyrs, detainees, and prisoners learn to work and support their families. The two silver hooks in the hand hurry along like two love birds exchanging happy kisses. Two hooks, pulling behind them a thread of wonderful color, trying to escape from it and escaping only into the bright woolen bedspread or the shawl that hints of the warmth of the body. At another table the fingers of the girls move with the needle that mixes color with color and stitch with stitch for many weeks, to take a form that grows day by day on the fabric, to emerge in the end as a Palestinian dress embroidered with tens of thousands of astonishing, brilliant units. Carvings of olive wood, of silver, of wax, of glass, mirrors in embroidered frames, clothes for children and men and women, a vast kitchen producing hundreds of meals of every kind for families where both partners work outside the home, a piano, a lute, a flute, a *dabka*, songs, dance troupes, and many, many other activities. For more than thirty years the Society has been helping those in need. Its funds come from wealthy Palestinian businessmen and from some Arab countries. Umm Khalil had established the Society two years before Ramallah fell to the Israeli Occupation in 1967. My tour started with the Museum of Palestinian Folk Art that the Society was getting ready to inaugurate after a few days, and ended with a wonderful surprise when the children's chorus performed for me, with Mrs. Tarazi accompanying them on the piano. This example of persevering local endeavor has attracted the attention of Palestinians throughout the land, not simply in Ramallah and Bireh. The Society has succeeded in creating jobs for those in need. It has nurtured and developed the talents of hundreds of children. It is a proof of the effectiveness of local initiative, for it is the locals who are most aware of their own reality, its circumstances, and its ever-changing needs.

In the evening I went on the promised outing into the Ramallah night with Walid and Saji. I had gone out with Abu Ya'qub and Wasim once and with Anis and Husam more than once, and I had been out on my own twice. Anyone who saw us wandering around the streets of Ramallah or talking across a table in one of its coffeeshops would have thought we were just a happy group of friends from the way we laughed out loud. Things are more complex than they seem.

This, then, is Ramallah of the nineties, not Ramallah of the sixties. I would not have understood its new details without my friends' explanations. It is natural that the look of the city should change in the eye of one who has been absent for a long time. My friends are troubled by the concrete high-rises that have appeared everywhere. Ramallah, for its people, is the houses roofed with apricot-colored tiles and the gardens surrounding them, the parks with their fountains, Broadcasting Street (or Lovers' Street, as we used to call it) with its high trees on either side, looking over green hills that ended on the Palestinian coast, whose lights twinkled on clear nights. I did not share their troubled feelings—this is the way of development and the price for the growth of the city. In fact, our hatred of the Occupation is essentially because it arrests the growth of our cities, of our societies, of our lives. It hinders their natural development.

On this outing, and the others before it, I saw most of my places. Ramallah Secondary School, its playing fields, its library in which I read *Kitab al-aghani*, its arched corridors. Old Ramallah. Batn al-Hawa. The Church of God. The Nablus Road. The Mosque of Gamal 'Abd al-Nasser. Al-Manara Square. I asked about Na'um Park. They said it had gone. In its place was a tall building and lots of shops.

I could not recognize the houses of Fuad Tannous, 'Adel al-Najjar, and Basim Khouri, whom I had shared a flat with in Cairo in my third year at university. But I recognized the house of Rami al-Nashashibi, our fourth comrade, because he lived in the same building as 'Omar al-Salih al-Barghouti, opposite the house of *Khali* Abu Fakhri.

One of the beautiful things about Ramallah is that its society is hospitable and transparent. Its texture is Christian–Islamic, the rituals of both religions mixing in it in a spontaneous fashion. The streets, shops, and institutions of the city are all decorated for

Christmas and the New Year, Ramadan and 'Id al-Fitr, Palm Sunday and 'Id al-Adha. Ramallah does not know creeds and factions. Ramallah Park and Rukab's ice cream—you can taste it simply by hearing its name or seeing the letters of its name on an advertisement. The Palestinian police manage the traffic well and disperse its jams at al-Manara Square. It is said that when the Occupation banned the municipalities the city turned into a rubbish dump, but cleanliness has come back now as we always knew it, a feature of Ramallah. There is less green now since Israel has been stealing the water since 1967, but even so the green still resists.

Talk of politics—and trying to guess what will happen next—never ends. It will remain thus for a long time. Politics have entered into the most miniature details of the souls of our men and our women since the Zionist project started knocking on the glass of our windows with its sharp nails and then on the doors, which it kicked down to enter all the rooms of the house and throw us out into the desert.

But even this situation does not justify the overt political approach of Palestinian poetry, in the homeland or in the Diaspora. Comedy is also necessary for Arab and Palestinian writing. Our tragedy cannot produce only tragic writing. We are also living in a time of historical and geographical farce. Palestinian painters living in the homeland have managed to avoid this trap and have produced excellent work, without ignoring the requirements and the specificity of the general situation. Everywhere I went I heard complaints about the unavailability of books printed outside Palestine, about people's isolation from Arab culture, from world culture, about the absence of opportunities to make contact with other Arab writers.

The Palestinian has his joys too. He has his pleasures alongside his sorrows. He has the amazing contradictions of life, because he is a living creature before being the son of the eight o'clock news. You meet these contradictions in the stories of the Intifada people tell: there was one chap who since we were children in Deir Ghassanah we had known for his burnt cheek. He used to argue with Yusuf al-Jabin, the village barber, that he should get a 50 percent discount because he only shaved one side of his face. He traveled to the Emirates to visit relatives and regaled their guests with stories of how his face got burnt in the Intifada. This was his send-up of the media stories that were fabricated to empty the Intifada of its content.

I remember now the documentary that was produced by Anis al-Barghouti (from the village of 'Aboud) about Farha, a peasant woman from their village: throughout the years of the Intifada, when women saw a young man captured by Israeli soldiers, they would attack the soldiers, all of them crying and screaming: "My son, my son—leave my son alone." On this occasion the soldier, dragging the young man away, shouts at Farha: "Go, you liar. How many mothers for one boy! A hundred mothers for one boy? Get away from here, go!"

She screams at him: "Yes, we're like that. A boy here has a hundred mothers, not like your kids, every boy has a hundred fathers!"

The phenomenon of the Palestinian woman in the Intifada deserves unhesitating admiration, but her complete story has not been written yet. People also tell of that woman in whose house a Palestinian fugitive took refuge: she hid him for seven years. They tell of the wanted men hiding in the mountains, of home agriculture and social solidarity, and of the small daily sacrifices that form the backbone of what we intellectuals call 'heroism.' They speak of the secret surgical operations carried out by volunteer doctors on those injured in the Intifada so that they would not be arrested from within the hospital.

And besides all this, they speak of the collaborators who cooperated with Israel in return for a few piasters or some simple perks. Israel now faces the problem of organizing the safe future it had promised for them and their families. They tell also of the summary, unrecorded midnight trials carried out by the Palestinian Security Forces, of commercial agencies and exaggerated profits, of the signs of economic corruption accompanying the process of redevelopment and construction. But the pressure of their hope (and hope pressures just as pain does) makes them add often during their speech that such irregularities are natural and expected in the beginning. Hope tells them that all the negatives will end once this difficult stage is over. The majority who gave their voice to Yasser 'Arafat are a real majority. But they are a majority who believed in the historic promises they were given and are waiting for them to be fulfilled. It is accurate to say that Palestinian society as a whole is still waiting. It has not closed its eyes yet. What surprised me was that the Palestinian media do not reflect this reality at all. They are too busy covering reality with flowers.

Walid was constantly returning the greeting of young men or women wherever we went. He sings and plays the lute and works in the theater, and he has never left Ramallah. This is a young girl from the theater, this young man trains in the dancing group, this is our old neighbor, and so on. We talked about the value of all this: the value of the writer or the artist being essentially the child of his own horizon. In these strange days of ours the Arab writer pants after the chance to be translated (specifically into Western languages) in order to raise his local value, as though he wants the English to read him so that the Arabs may know him. It is funny and sad. I wonder if it is happening with other nations now.

The three cinema houses closed down many years ago. The billboards are torn down, the areas surrounding them are dark. Bookshops do not sell books, they sell general things—sweets, and simple school implements (pens, papers, etc.). Car license plates are a variety of shapes and colors: some carry Hebrew codes and some Arabic. For a newly arrived naive like me it was difficult to work all this out. Walid spoke about his experiments in the theater, Abu Ya'qub about his work in the aid organization, Saji about abandoning political work and taking a job with an insurance company. Wasim spoke of the beautiful house with the tiled roof that the Ministry of Culture had restored and made into the 'Khalil al-Sakakini Cultural Center.' It will be a home for theater groups, artists, workshops, and a library, and *al-Karmel* magazine will occupy one of its floors. They took me to see the house.

I watched Palestinian television programs for the first time here. Throughout these last years we would name the things that—as refugees in other people's countries—we did not have: Palestinian airlines, Palestinian police, Palestinian television, Palestinian government. The television is content with everything, like all Arab television and radio. In a radio interview in Ramallah, my host asked me: "Are we not a miraculous people, a different people, a different nation?" I said: "Different from whom exactly? Different from what?" All peoples love their homelands and all peoples fight for their homelands if they have to. Martyrs fall for their just causes everywhere. Prisons and detention centers are crowded with the fighters of the Third World, and the Arab world is at their head. We have suffered and we have sacrificed without limit, but we are no better or worse than the others. Our country is beautiful and so are the countries of others. It is the relationship between people and their countries that makes it different. If it is a relationship of exploitation, bribery, and corruption, of course that affects the image of the homeland. When he asked what I thought were the conditions for a successful broadcasting service, I said it has to keep its distance from the governing powers.

In my room, before I fell asleep, I looked over the drafts of the text I was preparing for publication under the title "The Logic of Beings." I was given pause by what seemed a somewhat exaggerated use of comedy. But I said why not, let it be, it is like this. It is a tragedy, yes, it is a comedy, yes, I mean at the same time. In every dialogue the funny and the sad met in the same sentence. I do not believe an eye that ignores the comedy within the tragedy. It is always more comfortable to present tragedy as what happens to us rather than what our hands do. The situation is tragic but the tragedy is always tinged with comedy because it is without majesty. We fall silently, without that resounding noise that accompanies the fall of the hero in Greek or Shakespearean tragedy. The diabolic media machine fudges the meaning of the fall and presents it to us as a victory or a renaissance. This was not available in old tragedies. Hamlet said: "Something is rotten in the state of Denmark," and that was the end of it. You did not wake up next morning to a radio or TV program telling you that William Shakespeare was a trivial man with his own agenda and with no relationship to the struggle of the people, and that everything in Denmark is just fine, especially its wise leadership. You will not find an essay in the morning newspapers of the north that places its arms akimbo and yells in the face of poor William, son of Mrs. Umm William: "And what is the alternative, Mr. Shakespeare?" Did Anwar al-Sadat not say that he would applaud anyone who managed to do better than he did with his historic initiative? If only Oedipus had the eloquence to extract himself from his tragedies with such simplicity. But Oedipus cannot transform the catastrophe into a carnival or a festival. When Shakespeare wanted to write tragedy, he wrote tragedy; when he wanted to write comedy he wrote something completely different from *Hamlet* or *Lear* or *Macbeth* or *Othello*. We Arabs have become used to reading the tragedy and the comedy on the same page, in the same event, and in the same treaty, in the same speech, in defeat and in victory, in weddings and funerals, homeland and exile, and in the features of our one face every morning.

With the exodus from Beirut, after the Israeli invasion, Palestinian officials put more of a triumphal note into their general discourse. At the next meeting of the Palestine National Council they pushed up the level of the language of glory, resistance, and victory.

At the meeting of the Cultural Committee of the Council I thought that what I was saying would be shocking for the Palestinian cultural and media bureaucracy. "History has taught us two lessons: the first is that it is possible to present disasters and losses as victories. The second is that that cannot last."

I added: "Applauding ourselves is not a viable response to what has happened to us, and it does not help us to understand it."

In those days it was not permissible to violate the general contentment. It was not permissible to bring back and examine the phases of a chain of events and its results. In fact, I am not sure if it is permissible today.

Wrongdoers are immune to criticism. They were not shocked by what I said but they did not like it. When the meeting was over and all the participants were getting ready to go back to where they came from I bumped into one woman delegate who lived in Cairo. I wanted to send a letter to Radwa and Tamim before I went back to Budapest, and I thought she would take the letter for me. She said: "I'm not going directly to Cairo. I thought while I am close to France, why don't I go for a few days to Paris just for a change. One is so fed up. I want to buy some silver. I really love silver and I might stay a while in Paris. It depends. Just for a change."

The greater body of Palestinian intellectuals fell in line with the Authority, got closer to it than was wise, rested on its seats, took pleasure in imitating it and identifying with its features. People who supported the Authority and people who opposed it were similar in this respect. We still behave like a tribe. We were able to do so because the nature of the cause placed everyone, whatever their choices, among the patriots. Even those who did wrong could be seen as victims too. All are threatened, all are exposed to death or injury or humiliation at the border or the loss of a loved one. There was a constant feeling that the closeness of an intellectual to the leadership was different from being close to a traditional government. The Palestinian and his Authority both live the same exceptional situation, whether in exile or under occupation. Some would even say that the natural place for the Palestinian intellectual was close to the leadership, but the results of this choice were not always positive. There is also the question of personal predilection to corruption.

My own defect was that I find it too easy to retreat when I see something I do not like. I turn my back. The days have proved to me that it would have been better if I had put up with a little more and tried a lot more. I marginalized myself in order to put a distance between myself and the slightest hint of cultural or political despotism. The intellectual's despotism is the same as the despotism of the politicians of both sides, the Authority and the opposition. The leadership of both share the same features. They stay in their positions forever, they are impatient with criticism, they prohibit questioning from any source, and they are absolutely sure that they are always right, always creative, knowledgeable, pleasant, suitable, and deserving, as they are and where they are.

The image before the return of the PLO was the image of the freedom fighter, the image of the hero/victim who deserves sympathy and admiration. Now here is that same freedom fighter (chained with the conditions of his enemies), exercising his direct authority on the ordinary citizen, on the old men, on the students and the shops and the traffic and the customs and excise and arts and letters, taxes, courts, investments, and all the media. Livings and jobs from cleaner to cabinet minister are in his gift. It is he who determines social standing and influence. He mends what is broken, rebuilds what is ruined, and chooses his supporters and his enemies from among the people. Why, he even arrests citizens sometimes, imprisons them, and . . . tortures them.

This image is completely new to our people. This change in the function of the Palestinian could have been seen as an understandable or even a desirable development if it signified a true mastery over the Palestinian destiny. Nobody fights forever and nobody sings forever, but the cartoon control that we are permitted in our new situation and the bands that tie the decisions of the National Authority have had a different effect.

The song retreats and reality moves forward with its cruel

demands. In the cultural sphere as in others you will find those who are good at their work and perform it honorably and effectively out of conviction. Those who object to the injustice of the Oslo agreement but put all their capabilities faithfully at the disposal of the new Palestinian community to try and create what is less bad than the bad that is available. But you will also find the one who hops between positions and ideologies like a chimpanzee to reach the highest branch of the tree. Yet this is a chimpanzee who is good at choosing French perfume and stating his commission. He loves his children, his mother, his father, and (maybe) his wife—and no one else. This is a chimp that supports, then opposes, then supports while wanting to appear as though in opposition. Then he splits from his organization and forms a faction or a party to be added to the unnecessary crowds of factions and parties, and preaches on the necessity of unity. He may be content or disgruntled, he may humiliate himself in front of this one and act like a lion in front of that, but in every case he is brilliant at serving himself. Life, as you see, will not be simplified.

I said to Abu Hazim, by way of asking permission: "Today is the international day of telephones."

I wanted to call my mother in Amman and Radwa and Tamim in Cairo. They had called me practically every day and I wanted to take the initiative this time especially since I had news to tell them.

The Palestinian has become a telephonic person, living by the sound of voices carried to him across huge distances. Before the telephone became available to most people they used the broadcasting services. "All well, and you?" Then the wonderful, terrifying telephone came. "So-and-so passed his final exam." "So-and-so, we took her to hospital, but don't worry—it's nothing serious."

"So-and-so has passed away, may the rest of his days be added to yours,"

At one-thirty in the morning Mounif informed me from Qatar of the death of my father in Amman. I was in Budapest. At two-fifteen in the afternoon, seven years later, my brother 'Alaa informed me from Qatar of the death of Mounif in Paris. I was in Cairo.

The details of the lives of all whom we love, the fluctuations of their fortunes in this world, all began with the ringing of the phone. A ring for joy, a ring for sorrow, a ring for yearning. Quarrels, reproach, blame, and apology between Palestinians are introduced by the ringing of the phone. We have never loved a sound so much, and we have never been so terrified by one—I mean, at the same time. Bodyguards—or your luck, or your intelligence—can protect you from terrorism, but the displaced person can never be protected from the terrorism of the telephone.

But something good has happened: Abu Saji came himself to Abu Hazim's house and brought me the Palestinian identity card.

"Give me a few days for Tamim's entry permit . . . "

We had to manage our lives in those strange days, I in Budapest, Radwa and Tamim in Cairo. The university gave Radwa leave to accompany her husband, and she and Tamim came to live with me in Hungary. We put Tamim in Mani Nini's private nursery school, then in the nursery school of a stocking factory. At the beginning of September 1981 our friend 'Awatif 'Abd al-Rahman arrived in Budapest to visit us. She came from Berlin, where she had been at a conference. She stayed two days with us, then we took her to Budapest Airport to travel back to Berlin, then Cairo. We learned from the radio and newspapers that Sadat had arrested 1,536 men and women of all political persuasions who had not expressed their admiration for his 'historic initiative.' We read the names. It was natural that among the detainees would be all our friends in Egypt, and among them 'Awatif. We tried to call to warn her against traveling to Egypt and to invite her to stay with us until things became clearer. We knew she would be arrested at Cairo airport if she returned as planned. But it was too late. Our friend Fathi 'Abd al-Fattah's voice on the telephone: "'Awatif has gone. She's on the plane to Cairo right now." Two days later we received the expected news: 'Awatif was taken from the airport to prison. But the incident was not without its comic side: her duty-free purchases, particularly the Swiss chocolates, were very welcome to her cellmates: Latifa al-Zayyat, Amina Rashid, Safinaz Qazim, Farida al-Naqash, Shahinda.

News came thick and fast from Egypt: Sadat fires more than sixty journalists from their newspapers and moves a similar number of university professors to jobs outside education, among them Radwa. In Budapest we read the news of her transfer to the Ministry of Tourism. "You'll get your tips in shekels," I say to her. A month later we hear on the radio the news of Sadat's assassination. The events continue: the detainees are set free, the university teachers and the journalists are reinstated in their jobs.

A decisive moment came when we discussed Tamim's school. We took the decision: it was difficult and right. I said to Radwa: "Tamim has to be attached to the stable party in this family." Radwa had a stable homeland, a job, and a passport, and in Cairo we had a house, rented but still our home. More importantly, we wanted Tamim to be educated in an Arab country, not in Hungary. My position was temporary—temporary in every country, as was my work and as were my passports. Tamim's place was with Radwa, and Radwa's place was in her university, in her country, in our home.

From the moment we took that decision our small family was reunited for three weeks in the winter and three months in the summer, from my deportation in 1977 until Tamim was a young man in his final year of high school.

In the summer of 1984, seven whole years after I was deported from Egypt, I obtained a permit to visit Cairo for two weeks. And then I received an invitation to read my poetry at the Cairo International Book Fair.

The invitations to the Book Fair were repeated. I found myself also reading my poems at the Cairo University Faculty Club headquarters, at the Atelier, at the Journalists' Union, and at the Tagammu' Party.

On one of my visits to Cairo I was held at the airport and kept for a whole night in the veterinary quarantine—no, this is not a typographical error: the veterinary quarantine. On subsequent occasions they permitted me to be held in the luxury of the arrivals hall for periods that varied between five and twelve hours, before permitting me to enter Cairo. It was years later that the reason for this special treatment became clear. The cultural authorities welcome and the security authorities refuse: each time I arrived and until they could agree that I could enter, all those hours had to pass. I had to wait until the beginning of 1995 for them to get bored with stopping me, and for my entry at Cairo Airport to become as natural as the entry of a German, a Japanese, or an Italian.

I was putting questions to myself and answering them without much belief in the importance of either the question or the answer. When Tamim comes here, will he live as I have lived, a guest at Abu Hazim's? I should be with him then, but we will become two guests. But what's the sense in his coming alone? In theory we can be blamed for not having an apartment in Ramallah. The dictates of life, along with dozens of details important in their time, forgotten or remembered later, made the situation as it is now. The decisions of all the scattered families are taken, usually, on the basis of the needs of various members and on the basis of different interpretations of reality and different predictions for the future. Decisions are controlled by changing priorities that may not always be in the wisest order.

This boy—born by the Nile in Dr. Sharif Gohar's Hospital in Cairo to an Egyptian mother and a Palestinian father carrying a Jordanian passport—saw nothing of Palestine except its complete absence and its complete story. When I was deported from Egypt he was five months old; when Radwa brought him with her to meet me in a furnished flat in Budapest he was thirteen months old and called me 'Uncle.' I laugh and try to correct him. "I'm not 'Uncle,' Tamim, I'm 'Daddy.'" He calls me "Uncle Daddy."

7

DISPLACEMENTS

Displacements are always multiple. Displacements that collect around you and close the circle. You run, but the circle surrounds you. When it happens you become a stranger *in* your places and *to* your places at the same time. The displaced person becomes a stranger to his memories and so he tries to cling to them. He places himself above the actual and the passing. He places himself above them without noticing his certain fragility. And so he appears to people fragile and proud at the same time. It is enough for a person to go through the first experience of uprooting, to become uprooted forever. It is like slipping on the first step of a staircase. You tumble down to the end. It is also like the driving wheel breaking off in the hands of the driver. All the movement of the car will be haphazard and directionless. But the paradox is that strange cities are then never completely strange. Life dictates that the stranger acclimatize every day. This might be difficult at the beginning, but it becomes less difficult with the passage of days and years. Life does not like the grumbling of the living. It bribes them with different degrees of contentment and of acceptance of exceptional circumstances. This happens to the exiled, the stranger, the prisoner, and something like it happens to the loser, the defeated, the abandoned. And as the eye accustoms itself, little by little, to sudden darkness, they accustom themselves to the exceptional context imposed by their circumstances. If you become accustomed to the exception you see it in some way as natural. The stranger cannot plan for his long- or short-term future. Even plans for a single day become difficult, for some reason, but little by little he becomes used to improvising his life. His sense of his future and the future of his family is the sense of migrant workers: every period spent with the one he loves is short, however long it lasts. He knows what it is to be a secure lover and a scared loved one. He draws close when he is far away and feels distant when he is near. And he desires his two states and his two positions at the same time. Every home he has is the home of others too. His will is contingent on other wills. And if he is a poet, he is a stranger to 'here,' a stranger to any 'here' in the world. He strives to survive with his personal treasure despite his certain knowledge that his personal treasure might be worth nothing on the market.

Writing is a displacement, a displacement from the normal social contract. A displacement from the habitual, the pattern, and the ready form. A displacement from the common roads of love and the common roads of enmity. A displacement from the believing nature of the political party. A displacement from the idea of unconditional support. The poet strives to escape from the dominant used language, to a language that speaks itself for the first time. He strives to escape from the chains of the tribe, from its approvals and its taboos. If he succeeds in escaping and becomes free, he becomes a stranger at the same time. It is as though the poet is a stranger in the same degree as he is free. If a person is touched by poetry or art or literature in general, his soul throngs with these displacements and cannot be cured by anything, not even the homeland. He clings to his own way of receiving the world and his own way of transmitting it. It is unavoidable that he should be taken lightly by those who hold the ready recipes; those who live by the normal and the known; those who say he is 'moody,' 'changeable,' and 'unreliable,' and so on through all the adjectives stacked like pickles on their shelves; those who do not know anxiety, who deal with life with unseemly ease.

I had to concede that the telephone would be my permanent means of creating a relationship with a child of a few months. But I did not consider my deportation from Egypt a matter that warranted any feeling of bitterness. I would be foolish to complain of being afflicted merely by the dispersal of my family, while not one Palestinian family in Palestine or in the Diaspora was free of more cruel disasters.

The massacre of Tell al-Za'tar remains at the forefront of the memory, and periodically the demolition of houses on the West Bank and in Gaza is repeated. The Israeli detention centers are crowded with young and old. The injured do not find their medicine, even if they are lucky enough to reach any hospital. The climate of overcoming problems and accepting them as simple and bearable was the climate that we created, Radwa and I, whenever we spoke to Tamim, together or singly. This was the climate that helped him quickly to get rid of the feeling that he was an unlucky child. Radwa's wisdom and her care of Tamim in Cairo, along with my tendency to make jokes and funny comments, which he met with laughter that rang across the telephone—these helped him to live a happy and comfortable childhood.

The Hungarian exile was paradise for Tamim. Our home was a small apartment on the third and last floor of a pleasant building, among similar buildings, surrounded by a wall. It was not more than eighty square meters in extent and was situated on the enchanting Rose Hill, overlooking the Danube. Our apartment had a small balcony with wrought-iron railings, on which I hung rectangular flowerpots with red geraniums. I gave them so much love and care that Tamim said to me once: "You spend more time with your *mushkatli* more than you do with me and Mama." (*Mushkatli* is the Hungarian for geraniums.)

The house had a huge garden that sloped down with the hill. At its center were swings and two sandpits for the children of the district. It had two tall poplar trees that stood very close together, one slightly shorter than the other. The first thing Tamim cared about when he arrived was to make certain they were there in their place. He would hurry to the window of his small room to look at them. At the end of the garden there was an apple tree, with children always climbing its branches and playing on the pistachio-green grass underneath it, as though it bore both apples and children. Tamim was able to ride his tricycle as he pleased, without any danger, as long as he was within the large gates and in the garden, but still we would look out from the kitchen window to make sure he was all right. And if the snow fell while he was in Budapest in his mid-year holiday it turned every minute of his day into a festival. I used to see what Budapest gave him and say to myself that we owed it to our places of exile to remember the good things, if we did not wish to lie.

In this beautiful home, in this happy natural scene, as you look out every day at this green bursting with life, your telephone rings one night and a hesitating voice tells you that so-and-so died "half an hour ago." You discover that you cannot join in the funeral, accompany him to the grave, because you have no passport, or no visa, or no residence, or because you are forbidden from entry. At one-thirty in the morning Mounif's voice came to me across the phone— my father had died. I learned later that he had had his supper and gone to bed. My mother woke to the sound of a great cry, then everything was over. I did not know what to do with myself. I forgot completely what morning does in Budapest—does it come every day?

> *And the night around me does not pass,*
> *And no one around me to share my hurt and lie (truthfully)*
> *For my soul,*
> *Or blame my fragility so that I might blame him,*
> *And the distance between my loved ones and me*
> *Is uglier than a government.*

At school Tamim's personality evolved as a bright boy with a good sense of humor. Before he was two years old he surprised us by giving a speech imitating President Anwar al-Sadat, repeating some of his well-known phrases: "I'll make mincemeat of him!" and *"Bismilla-a-ah,"* and others that I have forgotten now. He would come back every day from the Hurriya School in Giza with a good collection of jokes that he had learnt from his Egyptian classmates.

"Wait, wait! Give me paper and a pen so I don't forget them before I get back to Nazareth." This was Naila's cry for help on an evening we spent with her and Tawfiq Zayyad in Cairo a few years ago, and she began making notes on the jokes that came thick and fast.

135

He knows all the stories of Deir Ghassanah, the stories of the guesthouse, and the news of the old men and women. He tells them in their peasant dialect exactly as though he had been born in Dar Ra'd. His sorrowful anger at the cutting down of the fig tree was more than the anger of the whole family. He will not forgive my uncle's poor wife what she did to a tree that he had never seen with his own eyes nor eaten the fruit of, but he cannot imagine Dar Ra'd without it.

He knows your veranda, Abu Hazim, with everything in it. He can tell you exactly where the photograph of his uncle Mounif is hanging.

This boy, who saw the light for the first time in the district of Manyal in Cairo, the capital of the Arab Republic of Egypt, and who speaks to us at home in Egyptian dialect, and who has seen nothing of Palestine throughout his twenty years, burns to see it like a refugee grown old in a distant camp.

He writes verses in *mijana* and *'ataaba* form. He throws aside his political science textbook and comes to my study with joyful eyes, takes hold of the lute that Radwa brought him—under the instructions of Nazih Abu 'Afash—from Damascus, and starts to sing as though he were al-Huzruq, the old singer of Deir Ghassanah.

I took part in a poetry evening in 1980 in Carthage, where Marcel Khalifa and I bought him his first lute. He was three years old, and the lute was the size of a small doll, but Marcel tried it in the shop selling traditional Tunisian crafts and said that it was a real lute, despite its absurd size. In Cairo, Radwa got him a tutor, Mr. Mahmud, who made him a slightly bigger lute. He continued his studies under Mr. Taymur, and then Mr. Adib. He is still with him. Emil Habibi used to joke with him: "Why didn't you turn out to be a terrorist like your father?"

I asked Abu Saji again how long he expected it to be before we could get Tamim's permit. He said they took their time issuing permits to young people. They were easier with the elderly, with those over fifty. The word 'fifty' rang in my ears like a coffee cup breaking on marble before the guest's fingers have even touched it. I feel that I have lived long and lived little. I am a child and an elderly man at the same time.

We were seven years late bringing Tamim into this world. We married in 1970 and decided from the beginning to postpone having children (until things become clearer). We did not know what those things were that we were waiting for to become clearer. Our general situation, or our financial situation, or our political or literary or academic situation? Radwa completed her MA at Cairo University two years after we were married. She then went on a government study mission to Amherst, Massachusetts, to study African-American literature as part of her university career.

Muhammad 'Ouda, when he was asked by a mutual friend whom he met outside Egypt about our news, Radwa and I, and whether we had any children yet, replied: "Radwa and Mourid have decided to postpone having children until the Middle East problem has been solved."

When she came back with her PhD in 1975 we felt that the time had come for some kind of family stability. She became pregnant and miscarried in 1976, then she became pregnant again and we were given Tamim on June 13 1977. The birth was difficult. I saw the pain of giving birth and felt that it was unjust that children were not named after their mothers. I do not know how men have stolen the right to name children after themselves. That feeling was not simply a temporary reaction to seeing a mother suffer during delivery. I still believe that every child is the son of his mother. That is justice. I said to Radwa as we took our first steps out of the door of the hospital, she carrying the two-day-old Tamim on her arm, "Tamim is all yours. I am ashamed that he will carry my name and not yours on his birth certificate."

And then the Egyptian president, Anwar al-Sadat, had a decisive role in defining our size as a family. His decision to deport me resulted in my remaining the father of an only child, Radwa and I not having a daughter, for example, to add to Tamim, or ten sons and daughters. I lived on one continent and Radwa on another: on her own she could not care for more than one child.

This is the permit then, the reunion permit. A green-plastic-covered card, holding my name, the name of Ramallah, the word 'married,' the word 'Tamim,' and a Palestinian stamp.

When Mounif left Qatar to live in France I visited him often. Entry visas were easy to get and he was near Budapest, where I was living. One summer I was taking part in an international symposium on Palestine for NGOs in Geneva. I took Radwa and Tamim and we stayed with Mounif at his home in Veigy Fonceneux, a village ten minutes' drive from Geneva. But going to Geneva (something that might be repeated several times in one day) meant crossing the border between France and Switzerland. Mostly the policeman would simply wave the driver on. Sometimes he decided to throw a quick glance over the passports before he smiled and sent the travelers on their way. That summer we were not the only guests staying at Mounif's. He was also host to some of his wife's relatives and their children and to two of her sisters. We drove across the border in two cars. The policeman stepped forward and asked for the passports. We collected them and gave them to him, and he saw an amazing sight: in his hands were passports from all over the world—Jordan, Syria, the United States, Algeria, Britain, and even Belize—and the names in all of them showed that their holders were from one family: all Barghoutis. Add to that Radwa's Egyptian passport and Emil Habibi's Israeli passport—for he had come from Nazareth to take part in the same Palestinian symposium in Geneva, and I had invited him to Mounif's house to eat *qatayef* in the land of the Franks.

I understood from the French speakers among us that the policeman asked for an explanation of this cocktail of travel documents, but when someone started to explain to him he interrupted, laughing: "That's enough! I don't want to understand."

He wished us a good time in Geneva. We continued on our way, carrying with us the Frenchman's surprise at our situation. Someone said: "You know, everybody, we really are a scandal."

Neither this ID nor even the new Palestinian passport that the Palestinian Authority has started to issue after the Oslo Agreement will solve our problems at borders. The states of the world acknowledge the Palestinian ID and the Palestinian passport on paper only. But at the borders, in airports, they tell the holder of these papers: "You have to be pre-approved by security." And this pre-approval we will never obtain.

Despite this, millions of refugees in the camps of the Diaspora are not allowed to carry the documents of the Palestinian Authority. They are not allowed to return to elect, to stand for election, to offer an opinion, or to have any political contribution. In Lebanon there is now a government decree prohibiting Palestinians resident in the camps from working in eighty-seven professions. In other words, they may only collect rubbish and shine shoes. Anyone who is allowed to travel out of Lebanon is not allowed to return to it. Is it believable that this should hold for more than a quarter of a million refugees of Palestinian origin, thousands of whom were born in Lebanon? And there are others who have lived in Lebanon since the thirties and forties of the twentieth century, that is, from before 1948, but their Palestinian roots cannot be forgiven. Some Palestinians wronged Lebanon. The children of the camps pay the price for this every day. If only all who had wronged Palestine would pay the price too! They say the question of the refugees and the displaced—that is, four million human beings—the questions of the settlements and Jerusalem, and the right to self-determination are all postponed to the final status negotiations. What is it that is urgent, then? I discussed this with most people whom I met and I picked up the answers of others in passing without posing the question. What is certain is that everybody is waiting, and that the movement of the soldiers of the Occupation away from their homes, even just a few hundred meters, gives them a sudden hope that in the future they will move away farther.

All eyes these days look at geography more than they look at history. Longings, desires, dreams postpone themselves for the moment. Palestine has turned into a daily workshop in which the workers are concerned only with the work they do here and now. But it may be noted—despite their impatience with general theories and analyses—that one can feel constantly the shadows of their suspicions of the intentions of Israel, its tricks and its coming surprises. There is hope colored with fear and doubt. Hardly anybody uses expressions such as 'victory.' Most people wait, tensely, and adapt—even though with difficulty—to the dictated reality. It is only those who have gained an immediate and direct material betterment from the new situation who see in it a victory that deserves dancing and celebration and who defend it unreservedly. I heard interesting comments from intellectuals who saw in the streets of the Intifada and in people's behavior during its first years a rare actualization of the national spirit, which was being shaped naturally every day, in spite of all the sacrifices.

Now the significations are confused. Abu Muhammad, one of our old neighbors, said to me: "Raising a small Palestinian flag on the roof of the school or a house or even on the electric wires on the street used to cost young men their lives. Rabin's army used to fire at anyone who tried to raise one flag, and we gave martyrs throughout the Intifada just to raise a flag. Now the flag is everywhere—behind the desk of every civil servant down to the smallest clerk."

"You don't like the fact that the romance has gone?"

"No, it's the absence of real sovereignty signified by the raised flag that I don't like. Israel will not let us have sovereignty even over transport. It still controls everything. You saw them on the bridge. What does the Palestinian side do on the bridge? Didn't you see? And hear?"

I saw and I heard.

He spoke about the continuous closures on the West Bank and in Gaza with a stroke of the Israeli government's pen: "They prevent even the leadership from traveling if they wish. You think you can go to Jerusalem, or even to Gaza. They've declared them enclosed areas, and their excuse this time is the elections. They stop people praying in the Holy Place even on Fridays. Barricades and searches and computers. They send us one message, all the time and in every way: 'We are the masters here.'"

"Was I wrong to come here, Abu Muhammad?"

"On the contrary. Anyone who can come back and live here should come back immediately. Should we leave it for the Falasha and the Russians and the Brooklyn Jews? Should we leave it to the settlers? Everyone should come back from abroad who can. With a permit, a reunion order, a job—anything. Build in your villages if you can. Build Palestinian settlements in Palestine. How can you ask if it was wrong? Come, my friend—come!"

He lit a new cigarette from the butt burning in his mouth: "But who told you the bastards have their eyes closed? They were forced to agree to allow a few thousand in because the world was watching, but I swear by your life, Abu Tamim, they've got it worked out. It's good you managed to get in, but I wish you had come before the closures. It's a shame that you won't see Jerusalem."

"Is it really impossible?"

"They think of Jerusalem as Israel. Closures mean that there is no movement between the Palestinian Authority areas and Israel, except for those who carry Israeli permits or a VIP card."

"And otherwise?"

"Smuggling. There are people who smuggle themselves in. It's a risk."

He was silent for a while and then said: "But after all this lifetime, are you really going to smuggle yourself into Jerusalem?"

All that the world knows of Jerusalem is the power of the symbol. The Dome of the Rock is what the eye sees, and so it sees Jerusalem and is satisfied. The Jerusalem of religions, the Jerusalem of politics, the Jerusalem of conflict is the Jerusalem of the world. But the world does not care for our Jerusalem, the Jerusalem of the people. The Jerusalem of houses and cobbled streets and spice markets, the Jerusalem of the Arab College, the Rashidiya School, and the

'Omariya School. The Jerusalem of the porters and the tourist guides who know just enough of every language to guarantee them three reasonable meals a day. The oil market and the sellers of antiques and mother-of-pearl and sesame cakes. The library, the doctor, the lawyer, the engineer, and the dressers of brides with high dowries. The terminals of the buses that trundle in every morning from all the villages with peasants come to buy and to sell. The Jerusalem of white cheese, of oil and olives and thyme, of baskets of figs and necklaces and leather and Salah al-Din Street. Our neighbor the nun, and her neighbor, the muezzin who was always in a hurry. The palm fronds in all the streets on Palm Sunday, the Jerusalem of houseplants, cobbled alleys, and narrow covered lanes. The Jerusalem of clothes-lines. This is the city of our senses, our bodies and our childhood. The Jerusalem that we walk in without much noticing its 'sacredness,' because we are in it, because it is us. We loiter or hurry in our sandals or our brown or black shoes, bargaining with the shopkeepers and buying new clothes for the *'Id*. We shop for Ramadan and pretend to fast and feel that secret pleasure when our adolescent bodies touch the bodies of the European girls on Easter Saturday. We share with them the darkness of the Church of the Holy Sepulcher and raise with them the white candles that they light. This is the ordinary Jerusalem. The city of our little moments that we forget quickly because we will not need to remember, and because they are ordinary like water is water and lightning is lightning. And as it slips from our hands it is elevated to a symbol, up there in the sky.

All conflicts prefer symbols. Jerusalem now is the Jerusalem of theology. The world is concerned with the 'status' of Jerusalem, the idea and the myth of Jerusalem, but our lives in Jerusalem and the Jerusalem of our lives do not concern it. The Jerusalem of the sky will live forever, but our life in it is threatened with extinction. They limit the number of Palestinians in the city, the number of Palestinian houses, the windows, balconies, schools, and nurseries, the number of people praying on Friday and Sunday. They tell the tourists where to buy their gifts, which lanes to walk in, which bazaars to enter. Now we cannot enter the city as tourists or students or old people. We cannot live there or leave there, we cannot get bored with Jerusalem and leave it for Nablus or Damascus or Baghdad or Cairo or America. We cannot desert it because of the high rents. We cannot grumble about it as people grumble about their tiresome capitals. Perhaps the worst thing about occupied cities is that their children cannot make fun of them. Who could make fun of Jerusalem! Now, letters to our addresses there will not reach us. They took the addresses of our homes and the dust of our drawers. They took the city's throngs and its doors and its lanes, they took even that secret brothel that stimulated our adolescent imaginations in Bab Hutta Alley, with its courtesans as fat as Indian statues. They took the St. Augusta Victoria Hospital and Jebel al-Tur, where *Khali* 'Ata lived, and the Sheikh Jarrah district where we lived once upon a time. They took the yawning of the pupils at their desks and their boredom in Tuesday's last lesson. They took the footsteps of my grandmother on her way to visit *Hajja* Hafiza and her daughter *Hajja* Rashida. They took those two women's prayers and their small room in the old city and the straw mat on which they used to play cards: *barjis* and *basra*. They took that shop I traveled to specially from Ramallah to buy a pair of quality leather shoes, to return to my family with cakes from Zalatimo and *kunafa* from Ja'far's: after sixteen kilometers in the Bamyeh bus for five piasters I went back to our house in Ramallah, proud and boastful—for I was returning from Jerusalem.

144

Now, I will not see either Jerusalem of the sky or Jerusalem of the clothes-lines. Israel, with the excuse of the sky, has occupied the land.

"A friend of yours called Abu Nail is on the phone," Abu Hazim called me. I hurried to answer. We agreed we would meet in Ramallah Park. I went with Husam and we found him already seated at a table in the crowded place. Husam asked: "How do you see the situation, Abu Nail?"

"I made up my mind without any hesitation when we were in Tunis. They said that under Oslo some people would be permitted to go back. When they asked what I thought I said: 'Listen, those who agree with Oslo belong there. The hypocrite belongs there. The opposition belongs there. Consider me in any category you wish— I shall go. It makes no difference to me whether I go to be in the Authority or in the street or in jail. I shall go. And here I am."

I offered him a cigarette. He said he had stopped smoking. I asked how he had managed.

"I hate changing cigarettes. You know, I used to smoke Rothmans. In the last years in Tunis Rothmans became very expensive, more than I could afford. I quit smoking altogether."

Husam asked what he did now. Abu Nail was for many years Palestinian ambassador to China, Ethiopia, and Italy. He said "I work in the Ministry of Social Affairs here in Ramallah." We went on to talk about literature. He expressed his admiration for Radwa's *Granada Trilogy* and naturally we moved on to poetry. He is a man of distinguished taste and an addicted reader.

"God help our people, man. No books, no libraries, no newspapers, no magazines. Everything is forbidden. Did you bring any of your volumes with you?" I had brought three copies of the latest collections. Suddenly, Sanduqa Bookshop sprang to my mind. It was near the Liftawi Building. I used to go in every day and squeeze among its shelves to look at the books. I loved their smell, their colors, and their feel. When I was a schoolboy I used to take a book from a shelf and look through it. If it pulled me I would read a few pages of it and put it back in its place, to return to it next day. That was how I read my first anthology of modern Arabic poetry. It had some poems by Badr Shakir al-Sayyab. They surprised me by the difference in their form, music, and atmosphere from the traditional poems I was trying to write in those days. And there I read pages of magazines and books about sex and marriage, and began to sense my maleness in these publications that had no counterpart in the family or the social dictionary that surrounded me. I used to see the novels of Naguib Mahfouz, Muhammad 'Abd al-Halim 'Abdullah, Yusuf al-Siba'i, and huge novels by Ihsan 'Abd al-Quddus. And the books of Ernest Hemingway, Jean-Paul Sartre, Simone de Beauvoir, Alberto Moravia, and Colin Wilson. And *al-Adab* magazine. My head would dive into the book like the head of a sheep in green grass, until the owner of the bookshop came to me one day and dragged me by the hand to his table. He stared into my face, then said: "Brother, have pity on me. By God, you spend more time in the bookshop than I do. What shall we do with you?"

After long days I went back and bought Hugo's *Les Miserables*, to show him that I was a solid and important reader and that I did not frequent his bookshop to amuse myself and look at the naked pictures only (although that of course was one of my secret aims). That night and the following day I read *Les Miserables*. This was the first book that I bought from my pocket money. It deprived me of the wonderful *shawarma* sandwiches whose smell flowed from

Abu Iskander's restaurant, which we visited every evening to avoid the repetitive family dinner and to feel that we were on an independent outing in the bright night of Ramallah.

How many talents have been broken since '48 in these lands? How many cities have wilted? How many homes have not been kept up? How many bookshops could have been set up in Ramallah, how many theaters? The Occupation kept the Palestinian village static and turned our cities back into villages. We do not weep for the mill of the village but for the bookshop and the library. We do not want to regain the past but to regain the future and to push tomorrow into the day after. Palestine's progress in the natural paths of its future was deliberately impeded, as though Israel wished to make of the whole Palestinian community a countryside for the city of Israel. More than that, it plans to turn every Arab city into a a rural hinterland for the Hebrew State.

Is it possible that I should go to the vegetable market in Ramallah, after an absence of thirty years to find it in the same decrepit state it was in thirty years ago, as though the stallholders had not changed their stalls, their clothes, or their price tags? Is it possible that I should find the ground here exactly as it used to be, like the surface of a marsh: sticky, dark, covered in skins and husks and colored mold? Is it possible that I should look at the facades of the buildings on the main street and find that they resemble the ground of the vegetable market?

I did not go to Jerusalem, to Tel Aviv or to any of the coastal cities, but everybody speaks of them as part of Europe in their organization, their green, their factories, and their produce. They moved forward as fast as they could and made sure that we would keep moving backward. I thought of this with everything I saw and with everything I heard. Here, it can be said that truths are concrete.

They build themselves on the dust of reality, not on the mirage of preconceived ideas. Here the idea returns to its body.

We left Ramallah Park. I went home with Husam on foot.

Ramallah, distributed over these green hills, has the feel of a village. The fact that it is connected directly to Bireh can give the impression that together they form a city, but the feel of life in Ramallah and Bireh together remains the feel of the countryside. The relationships of people to each other are rural relationships. Families know each other individually. Most of the passersby in its streets call each other by name. When a large number of people who had returned with the new Palestinian Authority gathered here, it started gradually to take on one of the features of the city, which is by its nature the meeting place for strangers. But the interesting thing about Ramallah or Bireh is that the strangers here are not strangers at all. They are the absent sons afflicted by displacement, the sons of the surrounding villages and the sons of the cities that have been lost since 1948, who chose to return and to live here in the suburbs that have started to expand. They live here because of the liberal tint of the social climate, because of the clement weather and the beauty of nature, and because geographically it almost abuts Jerusalem. And closeness to Jerusalem is a temporary substitute, for the probability is that Palestinians will be deprived of it in the end.

Husam said he might go to Amman in two weeks: "Suleiman's wedding. They've decided to have it in Amman."

"Which Suleiman?"

"Suha's nephew, man. Sameh's son."

"But Suleiman and his fiancée both live here, in the West Bank!"

"His aunts and his relatives and the relatives of his bride are outside, and his father's people are in Jerusalem. No permits and no visits. Meeting in Amman is easier for most people."

When I'tiqal (whose name means 'internment') married Robert in Budapest I thought that the homeland was the only medicine for the suppressed sorrow I detected she was trying to hide from me, from her groom and her guests. Is the homeland really the medicine for all sorrows? Are those who live in it less sad? I met I'tiqal in Budapest among the Iraqi refugees I got to know. On our second meeting she said to me: "You're the only person who hasn't joked about my name. Everyone who hears it asks me about it, except you. You just carried on talking without making me have to explain."

I said, laughing: "But you seem to want to explain!"

Anyway, we became friends. We stayed a long time in Hungary. I'tiqal graduated, then got a PhD in film studies, and did some translations for literary magazines in Budapest. She would sit by the hour, telling Radwa and me about her mother in Iraq, about her brothers, and about her displacement in Budapest. One day she came and told me she was getting married to a Hungarian lawyer named Robert, and that she wanted me to be her witness. I did not ask her why she had skipped over all her Iraqi compatriots in Hungary to come to me to help her get married. And so I found myself in the oddest situation for a stranger. I decked my car out with flowers and took her to the registry office in the 11th District in Budapest. I wore a formal dark blue suit and performed a role that is rarely required of a man still in his thirties. She wore the wedding dress that she had hired and held a small bouquet of yellow and white flowers. When we set off, a light evening rain shone in our headlights and we exchanged glances that told of the gratitude each of us felt toward the other—I, who have no sister, and I'tiqal, who was taking me to help her get married in this strange land. In front of the registry office the rain was coming down hard on our heads as we crossed the broad pavement.

Robert was very happy that evening and did not notice the tears that shone suddenly in his bride's eyes. She turned to me, the tears growing clearer: "My mother used to say to me: 'Don't let the water boil out of the pot, or else you'll get married in the rain.' You see, Mourid. It's raining."

We sat in front of the registrar, who wore the Hungarian flag across her chest. For a moment the whole scene seemed comic, but the tremor in I'tiqal's voice as she said in Hungarian "*Igen*" ('Yes') moved me immediately to a state where laughing was impossible. I signed the contract. We left the hall to have dinner in a restaurant with a few friends. Over dinner I'tiqal asked me: "Mourid, have you ever seen an Iraqi wedding in Iraq?"

On a visit to Budapest later, after I had left Hungary for good, I asked after I'tiqal and Robert and visited them. They introduced me to their only child, Hana, who said '*bazzuna*' for 'cat,' spoke to me in an Iraqi accent, and asked if I liked Carl Orff's *Carmina Burana*. I know very well that weddings in exile are not all like that. Some weddings in exile are extravagant and showy to an extreme degree, but I'tiqal's wedding was a lesson in loneliness and in the feeling that you are small, with no people, no traditions, and no history preceding your presence here and now. The thoughts that ran silently in the mind were cruel, hidden, leaving the floor for the declared joy. And the moment in the end was a moment of joy, not because of our condition but in spite of it. But I said nothing of this. Did I or she need to speak? Strangers meet with strangers and the experience of wounded Arabs taught me that my hurt as a Palestinian is only part of a larger whole. I learn not to exaggerate it. All those who have been destined to exile share the same features. For an exile, the habitual place and status of a person is lost. One who is known becomes anonymous, one who is generous has to watch what he spends, one who is merry gazes in silence. The fortunate ones are looked upon with suspicion, and envy becomes the profession of those who have no profession except watching others. Europe, where I lived for years, was full of them, from all the Arab countries. Each one had a story I cannot record, perhaps nobody can record. The calm of the place of exile and its wished-for safety is never completely realized. The homeland does not leave the body until the last moment, the moment of death.

The fish,
Even in the fisherman's net,
Still carries
The smell of the sea.

The stories of the wounded homelands are like the stories of the safe exiles: nothing in either place is done according to the wishes of the victims. I remember Michel Khleifi's film *The Wedding of Galilee*. It was filmed in Deir Ghassanah and tells the story of a wedding that is planned to be perfect, but events always develop in contradiction to wishes. We see that nothing can be carried out as planned in a reality like the reality in the film. The wounded reality, the reality of Occupation. In exile, the lump in the throat never ends: it is always resumed. In exile, we do not get rid of terror: it transforms into a fear of terror. And because those who are thrown

151

out of their countries are frustrated, and those who have escaped from their countries are frustrated, they cannot avoid tension and anger in their daily dealings among themselves. Their eyes are always alert to judge each other. Their warm feelings toward their people back in the homeland can only be consciously cooled down, so that a person who is naturally tender and sensitive may appear cruel. And when emotions are aroused for any reason, or even for no reason, then sadness will have its day.

Just as they have left behind a situation where things were not right, they discover that in exile too, things will not be right.

8

REUNION

We went back to find the house full of guests and Abu Hazim saying: "Where were you, man? We worried about you. Where did you take him, Husam? Radwa and Tamim called from Cairo and Umm Mounif called from Amman and the house is full. Lots of people asked after you on the phone."

I had asked Radwa to fax me a copy of Tamim's birth certificate to complete his application. I gave her the fax number of the Ministry of Culture. She assured me she had sent it. The following morning I went to collect the fax. I met my friends, Yahya Yakhluf, Mahmoud Shuqayr, Ali al-Khalili, and Walid. I was told that the Minister was there so I went in to see him. He was in a meeting with some people, among whom I knew Hanna Nasir, the president of Bir Zeit University. He greeted me, smiling: "So, the opposition's here!"

In the Ministry there was a long discussion about the position of Egyptian intellectuals toward normalization and the relationship with Israel. I said that their stand on this was wonderful and that it was to the advantage of the Palestinian cause that we support them, that we should be happy that they hold fast to their position. They are fighting the Arab and Egyptian cultural war, and they battle against the repercussions of Camp David and against the policies of Israel that are unjust to us here. We should not forget that the Egyptian student movement, which reached its height in 1972 with the sit-in in Cairo University, was born of the Society for the Support of the Palestinian Revolution at the Faculty of Engineering. The Palestinian cause was the pivot of the struggle and political activity of Egyptian youth, and the primary factor in shaping the destiny of many of them and in forming their intellectual and cultural make-up. I said too that the whole world exerts pressure on the Palestinians both in war and in peace, while nobody exerts pressure on Israel. We go to negotiate: we ask for a step from their prime minister and he refuses. We dig our heels in and leave the meeting and complain to our wives and to a few helpless journalists, while the prime minister of Israel leaves the negotiating table to sleep in Jerusalem. Which of us is in the more difficult situation? Does the enemy not deserve a little difficulty?

My friends asked me to give them a manuscript of some of my poems to publish, but I preferred that the first book to be published for me in my homeland should be a selection of my poetry rather than one particular volume of verse.

The rift between the displaced poet and his people is almost complete, and grows wider because books are banned. Israel used to prohibit the importation of most Palestinian literary works— fiction, prose, essays, whatever. Newspaper cuttings, Arab radio and TV programs, and the few contraband books smuggled in presented some kind of a solution.

I promised my friend Mahmoud Shuqayr that before I left I would leave a selection of poems with him. These were published a few months later by the Ministry of Culture in cooperation with al-Farouq Publishing House in Nablus. At last my voice, or part of it, returned to its place and its people.

I went to the Home Office and repeated my thanks to Abu Saji for his interest and gave him Tamim's birth certificate.

"Don't worry, insha'allah everything will be all right. Leave me your phone number and address in Amman or in Cairo and as soon as the approval comes I'll call you myself."

"You could call Anis, too. He knows where I am. But when do you think the approval will come?"

"It might be delayed. Are you in a big hurry?"

"Tamim is coming to Amman in two or three weeks. I'm going to Amman tomorrow. If the permit comes soon I can come back to Ramallah with Tamim. The important thing is to get the permit before the school year begins, since Tamim has to go back to university, as you know." I said goodbye and left.

Tamim will live here one day.

Once, I was taking part in a symposium in Vienna. I left my seat to do a quick interview with a newspaper and returned to find a woman sitting in my place. She was the Israeli laywer Felicia Langer, who specializes in defending Palestinian detainees. She turned, saw me standing, and said: "My God, we occupy Palestinian places even in Austria."

We were in the worst part of the eighties. The war in the refugee camps in Lebanon had reached its dirtiest stage. The PLO was fragmented, its factions engaged in a brutal war with each other. The martyrs of Sabra and Shatila were being killed a second time by the rifles of the Palestinian factions and their partisans. New martyrs were being added from Burj al-Barajneh: innocent people dying for no declared reason.

We were in a break between two panels. At the same table, in the lobby of the hotel, we sat: two leaders from the Lebanese National Movement, Mrs. Langer, Yevgeny Primakov (the Soviet expert in Arab affairs), and two friends from Sweden. Somebody came to tell us that the Mufti of Lebanon had said it was lawful for the people of the camps in Beirut to eat cats and dogs. I was not sure if this was a real piece of news or another cry for help over the media to put an end to that apparently endless hell. But the accumulated tension because of what had been going on in the camps over the past days, the absurdity of the fighting and the killing, brought back to me once again the feeling of the mingling of tragedy and comedy. I said to Felicia: "Where should we go? Would you accept me as a refugee in your country?" I was of course using this expression deliberately to try to find out how she regarded our country. I was in a sense referring to Israel's responsibility for our being in Sabra, Shatila and Burj al-Burajneh, for our being in the camps at all, for our being despite ourselves in the countries of others, for the shape of our entire fate, whether in Palestine or in the Diaspora. I expected (because of her known position and her support for us) that she should be upset, that she would contemplate my question for a little while and see what lay behind it. But she was completely unable to pick up the resounding bitterness in my question. Her answer came as a shock, as a slap in the face: "I wish! But the laws of our government would not permit it."

Israelis may feel sympathy for us but they finds enormous difficulty in feeling sympathy for our 'cause' and our story. They will exercise the compassion of the victor over the loser. In Palestine the symmetry between the two sides is complete: the place is for the enemy and the place is for us, the story is their story and the story is our story. I mean, at the same time.

But I cannot accept any talk of two equal rights to the land, for I do not accept a divinity in the heights running political life on this earth. Despite all this, I was never particularly interested in the theoretical discussions around who has the right to Palestine, because we did not lose Palestine in a debate, we lost it to force. When we were Palestine, we were not afraid of the Jews. We did not hate them, we did not make an enemy of them. Europe of the Middle Ages hated them, but not us. Ferdinand and Isabella hated them, but not us. Hitler hated them, but not us. But when they took our entire space and exiled us from it they put both us and themselves outside the law of equality. They became an enemy, they became strong; we became displaced and weak. They took the space with the power of the sacred and with the sacredness of power, with the imagination, and with geography. Can I hold on to Tamim's right to this space? Let him enter this summer, let him enter after two or three summers, let him enter after twenty summers—the important thing is that he should have the right to live here one day. Even if he should choose to live elsewhere after that. The stranger who can return to his first place is different from the stranger whose displacement plays with him without his having a say.

I examine my fatherhood to Tamim and remember my father's fatherhood to us. Perhaps he was more tender toward us? Or are we simply a generation that deliberately avoids showing all its emotions in front of anyone, even a son? Perhaps it is an evasion that stems from a different sensitivity, as though by suppressing any loud emotion we are putting forward a model of fortitude and the ability to face the surprises of time. We propose this model to our children and to ourselves. We choose the practical ways of expressing what goes on inside us and deliberately avoid encouraging emotional clarity in our children.

When I used to say goodbye to Radwa and Tamim at Budapest airport I would be unable to stop joking and talking at some volume about everything except the one thing that was on all our minds—their imminent departure. My father's or mother's farewell to any one of us, their children, was a scene heavy for us all. When we said goodbye to Mounif, who was traveling to work in Qatar, our mother suddenly fell down in a faint on the stone floor of Qalandiya airport. She lost consciousness and speech for minutes, terrifying us all. My father used to write me moving letters. It was impossible not to feel disturbed for some time after reading them. I treat Tamim as though he were a colleague or an equal. I am not even aware of how attached I am to him, except when I speak about him in his absence to friends. Even my daily interaction with Radwa is of a concealing nature that does not express emotion in language. She is "a mixture of beauties," I tell friends. I do not think I have ever said it to her. When I paint a poetic image of her, the poem becomes a listening to the self, not an address to her. I am surprised at people who carry photographs of their loved ones in their pockets or their wallets. If I do that it is for a purely practical reason. This time, for example, I brought several small photographs of Tamim to accompany the application for an ID.

When Latifa al-Zayyat visited the Fedayeen bases in Jordan in the late 1960s, her description of them when she returned to Cairo was marvelous. I asked: "How did you find the people there?"

She replied, laughing: "They are good ruffians."

Who has stolen our gentleness? Now, the good ruffians are the children of the Intifada. They are full of a kind of rough plain-speaking. The ones I met among family and friends I found less fearful, less awkward, and less reserved than us when we were their age. Their manual skills are amazing to a person like me, and their ability to debate and discuss and marshal evidence and tell stories surpasses the ability of their peers among the children of countries that live under normal circumstances. Is it because they have seen more? Because they have learned to bear responsibilities early?

Are they like this because their parents were occupied with matters more crucial than training them in shyness and deference? They speak of factions and parties. They say this one is Fatah, that one is Hamas, the other is Communist, the fourth is the Front. They know all the national songs and anthems and they can dance the *dabka*. They do not hesitate to perform when they are asked.

I do not want to say that they are geniuses or even particularly brilliant, but I am noting a sensibility very different from the sensibility of childhood as we lived it. My father used to call me sometimes in front of his guests to recite a school poem, for example, or even the multiplication tables, and I would be desperate to escape from the whole house, and invent every possible excuse to avoid the situation. But 'Habbub' sat close to me on the sofa on the veranda of his grandfather, Abu Hazim, and said, with no preliminaries: "Shall I sing you a song, *'Ammu*?" Another day he said to me: "I'm going to the shop to buy biscuits. What would you like me to buy you? I've got money." He took his money out of the pocket of his short trousers to prove the truth of his statement and added, after I had politely declined his offer: "I'm serious." I said: "I'm the one who wants to buy you a present. Tell me—what can I get you that would make you happy?" He answered quickly: "Come and sleep in our house. Why are you always staying in *Giddu* Abu Hazim's house?" I said to Abu Ya'qub that his son was very charming, and

159

I told him about his invitation and his enthusiasm to buy me something from the shops. He said, as he threw his son a glance that was part admiration, part puzzlement: "He's a troublesome boy. Every day he comes back from school with a problem. He's either beaten up a boy or driven a teacher mad."

Yes, perhaps this is what I want to say about the child of the Occupation: a complex personality, combining a certain transparency of the emotions with pushiness. Fear and boldness, fragility and insensitivity.

I wondered again about that rubbish they call the 'poetry of the stones' and the poems of solidarity with the 'children of the stones.' It is the simplification that takes the accessible and the easy from the human condition and so blurs that condition instead of defining it, misrepresents it at the moment of pretending to celebrate it. It is the eternal difference between profundity and shallowness. Between art and political rhetoric. And what is interesting is that the writers who lived under the Occupation and lived the Intifada fell into the same error as the writers of the Diaspora. They failed, like them, to penetrate to the essence of their material even while they were writing their lived experience. I said to myself that the heart of the matter was in a detailed knowledge of life, and of the human maturity that is the foundation for all artistic maturity. These are features that no work of art worthy of the name can do without, whatever the lived experience. What is important is the piercing insight and the special sensitivity with which we receive experience, not simply our presence at the event, which, important as it is, is not enough to create art. Art has conditions, art is greedy. We lived the experience of our displacement in the lands of others, and we lived with other displaced people who looked like us. Did we write our displacement? Why should our story, our particular story deserve to be listened to by the world? And who listens to the stories of those men, women, and children who are taken by their displacement to that other shore from which no one ever returns? Our dead are scattered in every land. Sometimes we did not know where to go with their corpses; the capitals of the world refuse to receive us as corpses as they refuse to receive us alive. And if the dead by displacement and the dead by weapons and the dead by longing and the dead by simple death are martyrs, and if poems are true and each martyr is a rose, we can claim to have made a garden of the world.

This is my final night in Ramallah. I put in the application for a reunion permit for Tamim and felt that this step in itself was an achievement. The day passed crowded with guests: family, friends, neighbors, and colleagues. The conversation flowed and I tried to be the one who listened, who did not speak. Later, I took the manuscript of "The Logic of Beings" and went to bed.

In the room the silence was complete, as though it were a circle drawn in a book. For a while now I have preferred listening. "The Logic of Beings" is built on the idea that creatures—inanimate, plant, animal, or human—'speak.' My role is to listen to what they say. In my first volume of poems I proposed to humanity nothing less than the deluge and new genesis. I was in my twenties, a suitable age to be certain of your wisdom.

I wrote poetry at university and then in Kuwait, where *Khali* 'Ata made me go when I met him in Egypt in '67. I was looking for ways to avoid staying there. I wanted to carry on working with poetry and with literature. I published in *al-Adab, Mawaqif,* and *al-Katib* magazines.

To Radwa goes the credit for our decision to leave Kuwait permanently and return to Cairo. We got married in 1970, then after less than a year we left Kuwait. We went to Beirut, planning to stay there for a few days before taking the boat to Alexandria. We stayed in the al-Hamra Hotel. From the cover of a volume of poetry I took the telephone number of Dar al-'Awda publishing house.

"Hello? Mr. Ahmad Sa'id Muhammadiya?"

"Yes?"

"My name is Mourid al-Barghouti and . . ."

"Welcome, poet! Are you calling from Beirut?"

Radwa was with me in the room. I put my hand over the mouthpiece and said to her: "He says 'Welcome, poet'!"

I thought I needed a long and clever introduction to ask for an appointment and persuade him to publish my first collection in the well-known publishing house he owned and ran. I thought, living in Kuwait, that nobody in Beirut, the capital of Arab publishing, had heard of me. I said: "I'm in the al-Hamra Hotel."

"Come and have a cup of coffee. You must have a manuscript—bring it with you."

Within minutes he had agreed to publish it, and it came out in January 1972. I had given a copy of the manuscript to Mona al-Su'udi to design a cover. She designed it but she put the name Mounif al-Barghouti instead of Mourid al-Barghouti. The publisher did not, of course, bother to redo the cover, and the collection appeared with Mounif's name hidden under a rectangle of silver ink and mine written on top of it. If you look closely you can still see the two names mixed together. For both him and me this mixing symbolized something special, which made it easier to bear the ugliness of the cover.

I try to sleep—I cannot sleep. I write a fragment here and a fragment there. Casual observations, summaries of a conversation. When I switch off the light and close my eyes the sounds of my life start rising in this quiet, dark room. Thoughts and questions and images from the life that is past and the life that awaits me, awaits us.

The involvements of the day turn at night into a heavy weight. Something wants to be completed. I try to measure the distance created by separation between those living there and those living here, between the living and the dead both here and there. I pick up the manuscript of "The Logic of Beings" and read:

He who is happy is happy at night;
He who is sad is sad at night.
As for the daytime,
It engages its people!

I tried to put the displacement between parentheses, to put a last period in a long sentence of the sadness of history, personal and public history. But I see nothing except commas. I want to sew the times together, I want to attach one moment to another, to attach childhood to age, to attach the present to the absent and all presents to all absences, to attach exiles to the homeland and to attach what I have imagined to what I see now. We have not lived together on our land and we have not died together. There, in the Gare du Nord in Paris, at 11 o'clock at night, Mounif staggered before he fell at the edge of the platform in the November frost to return to his mother and to us in a coffin. This man, who lived by his friends and for his friends, and who loved to fill his life with people—people coming and going, visiting, receiving, on the phone—was he preparing himself for this last day: a solitary, lonely, mysterious death in the Gare du Nord? November 8, 1993—Radwa, Tamim, and I at the lunch table in our home in Cairo. The telephone rang.

I went to answer. My younger brother 'Alaa's voice, speaking from Doha. His weeping voice said a few words I do not remember. A coldness ran through my shoulders. I do not remember what I said. What I remember clearly is that Radwa jumped out of her seat, her face pale, asking what had happened. I said: "Mounif is dead. Dead."

One of his friends had called from Geneva and said he had been in an accident in the Gare du Nord in Paris. I called his home and Geneva, trying to find out more. They said that he was alive and they were trying to save him. Then they said he had died. I lived in this confusion before phoning our mother in Amman. I realized they had told her only that he had been hurt in an accident. I said to Radwa: "My mother will not survive him."

I called Majid and 'Alaa in Doha. I asked them not to tell our mother about Mounif's death. I wanted to be at her side. I told Radwa that my only duty now was to protect my mother. I said: "If we manage to make her live two days after the news, she will live. The important thing is to get her past the moment of receiving the news."

I was dealing with the tragedy in a strange way, as though I had been thrown into an earthquake and come out looking for my mother's fate in it—as though I had succeeded in pushing aside the news itself, so that I could stay in control of events. Somebody had to stay in control of events. I was like someone who had been suddenly attacked and so suddenly transforms himself into an operations room, directing the response to this attack. I thought about everybody, about my mother, Mounif's children and his wife, my brothers. I had to concentrate on what could be done practically.

I asked Majid and 'Alaa in Doha to get entry visas to France and travel immediately to be near his family. It was impossible for me to obtain such a visa from Egypt. They went to Paris. The following day I went with Radwa and Tamim to Amman. Husam met us at the airport. He told us the details. Mounif had taken the train from his home to Paris. He did a few things, then went to the Gare du Nord to catch the 4:30 train to a meeting in Lille. He missed the train and waited in the station for the next train at 5 o'clock. At 11 o'clock the French police found him bleeding on the station platform. What stopped him getting on the 5 o'clock train? What kept him in the station for seven hours? Had he been kidnapped? Had he been attacked by thieves or shaved neo-Nazis? Was this a political assassination? He had been under treatment for many years for a liver disease. Had he been subject to a sudden coma and been attacked by a passerby who saw in him a victim easy to rob? The ambulance came and found him barely alive. They tried to save him but it was useless, he died moments later.

The owner of a coffee-shop at the station said he had been seen entering the coffee-shop, staggering and bleeding. The waiter thought he was drunk and pushed him out. He tried to go in again. He must have been trying to ask for help. Maybe he was trying to get to the telephone. He walked two or three steps and fell on a table where two young Portuguese men were sitting. The two young men got up and threw him out. Four steps outside the door of the coffee-shop he fell for the last time.

Husam gave us all these details, broken up, weeping. He said they had told my mother nothing. They told her he had been in a car crash but he was all right. He said Dr. Jihad and Dr. Muhammad were keeping her under observation. They said our house was full with all the women of the family who lived in Amman and that he had forbidden them to use words of condolence: "They all know, your mother is the only one who doesn't. Her heart feels the disaster but she's holding on to a word from you to give her hope. We've followed your instructions and not told her."

The door of our house was wide open. We went in. I looked into the drawing-room: some of the women were in black. My mother was sitting in a state of semi-consciousness, wearing a pale blue dress. The moment Radwa, Tamim, and I entered, the house exploded in wailing. I do not know how I avoided collapsing in those moments, but because I avoided it at that moment I was no longer vulnerable to it at any later time. My fear for my mother and my concern to protect her life preserved me too.

My mother had never had a daughter and she had no sisters. Radwa's presence in Amman was important. My mother had treated Radwa as a daughter since she saw her for the first time after we got married. I knew that Radwa's presence at her side at these moments would mean a great deal to her. I drew near and embraced her.

"Tell me, son, what happened to your brother? They are dressed in black and tell me he still has breath, he is alive in hospital and might get better. Tell me, my son. Don't lie to me, my darling."

I wanted my life to end there, at that moment. I did not know how to answer her. I found myself saying, as I put her head on my chest and held on to her very tightly: "We want you to stay alive. Promise me that you will stay alive. Put on black clothes, mother."

There, in Surrey, just outside London, he lies under the distant earth, away from the village of al-Shajara and from the camp of 'Ein al-Hilwa: Naji al-'Ali. Widad's brother said, as he sat next to me in the car that took us from Wimbledon along a curving road that ran through English woods as we followed the map to find the cemetery: "What brought us here, Mourid?"

I corrected him, saying: "What brought *him* here?"

Which cares were we carrying in that cemetery, the care of his small children or of Widad, or our care, the care of all our history and our story?

And there, at the bottom of that deserted well, in a wood on Visegrad mountain on the border between Hungary and Czechoslovakia, lies Luay. The good-looking, light-hearted young man who was doing well in his displacement in Hungary. He got a job running a holiday camp and a bar, there at the highest point of the mountain, which was covered all over with trees. He married a pretty, gentle, Hungarian girl and had two children with her. We used to go in the snow to this camp, which was forty kilometers from Budapest and he would hang a 'Closed' sign on the bar and we would cook bouillabaisse over the logs burning in the fireplace. We played cards or invited friends to an Arab supper. We threw snowballs. We collected mushrooms from the steep slope of the hill. His wife, who had learned a few words of Arabic, would help us cook them to the accompaniment of the music of Fayrouz.

Then, as he was considering joining a brother of his working in the United States, Luay vanished without a trace. His pleasant, friendly wife had shot him while he was watching television late at night. With the help of a Romanian petty criminal she dragged his body into the darkness of the wood and buried him in that deserted well. She covered his body with quantities of cement but it was later found by the police and she went to jail. Our friends used to look at Luay's life and see in him the happy, comfortable Palestinian, who was picky with his relationships, with food, and with his clothes—a Palestinian who was managing his life, forming a family, working hard, and saving some money. He cannot now from his dark well tell them that happiness lies. Security, good looks, and love—they all lie. Displacement gave him exactly what he had escaped from when he left southern Lebanon: death.

And there on the steps of the Middle East Airlines plane at Beirut airport, Abu'l-'Abd Darwish, Mounif's father-in-law, dropped dead on his way to visit his daughters in Qatar. His body lay for a week in a Lebanese morgue.

The telephone never stops ringing in the night of far-off countries. Someone woken from sleep picks up the receiver and hears a hesitant voice at the other end telling them of the death of a loved one or a relative or a friend or comrade in the homeland or in some other country—in Rome, Athens, Tunis, Cyprus, London, Paris, the United States, and on every bit of land we have been carried to, until death becomes like lettuce in the market, plentiful and cheap.

I said to Naji, as I watched his children playing in the hotel swimming pool: "Let's hope they wait a while till these kids grow up and you can leave them alone in this world."

The smell of his killing was getting stronger every day. The hate campaign against him tempted any silencer to exploit it. I feared for him.

He visited me in Budapest with his family when his young daughter, Judy, needed physiotherapy after being hit in the leg during the Israeli raids on Sidon. We spent a month together, and I did not see him again until I went to London several months later to visit his grave.

He wore shorts and sat next to me at the side of the swimming pool, his cigarette in his hand. You could count the ribs of his chest.

"You know, Mourid, I've thought about this, but it's not a problem. I asked myself, What did my father leave me when he died? Nothing, and even so I managed to live and sort myself out. They'll take care of themselves."

I got to know Naji in 1970 in Kuwait. He was the cartoonist of *al-Siyasa* newspaper, and I used to spend some evenings in his small office. I was working as a teacher in the technical college and preparing my first collection of poems for publication. I came to know him well and saw how one can touch talent with one's fingers. I saw also how courage can be as clear as a coffin.

We sat up most of the night talking, then I would leave him to draw his cartoon for the next day and wonder what he would draw. I would buy the newspaper in the morning and be surprised that that young man—puzzled, simple, laughing, sad—had summarized the world in his daily box better than any political analyst. Our friendship continued from one year to the next, from one country to the next. In 1980, at a poetry festival in Beirut Arab University, I wrote a poem entitled "Hanthala, the Child of Naji al-Ali." *Al-Safir* newspaper later published it on a whole page, surrounded by Naji's drawings.

Here everything is prepared as you would wish,
Something to suit every occasion:
A loudspeaker on the night of the festival,
A silencer on the night of the assassination.

Seven years after that night, the night of the assassination arrived. I was with Radwa and Tamim in a hotel on Lake Balaton in Hungary during our summer vacation. We woke up early and I switched on the radio to the BBC from London and picked up the end of a sentence about the "prominent Palestinian cartoonist." We knew immediately that Naji had gone. Tamim woke up as we fiddled with the radio to try to get more news: "Mama, Papa—what's the matter?"

"They've killed *'Ammu* Naji."

Naji was shot on July 22, 1987, coincidentally our wedding anniversary. Our private days were losing their meaning one by one as the events stretched out their rough hands to tear up our personal calendar and scatter it—tiny pieces of paper—to the wind.

Many years before that, at noon on Saturday July 8, 1972, my birthday, I was sitting in Broadcasting House in Maspero in Cairo, having just recorded a literary interview, when I saw Shaf'i Shalabi running down the stairs to tell me that Ghassan Kanafani had been murdered in Beirut. I went with Sulayman Fayyad to Yusuf Idris at his *al-Ahram* newspaper office. We said we wanted to hold a symbolic funeral for Ghassan Kanafani in Cairo at the same time as his funeral in Beirut. We met in the afternoon at Café Riche—Yusuf Idris, Naguib Surour, 'Abd al-Muhsin Taha Badr, Yahya al-Taher 'Abdallah, Sulayman Fayyad, Said al-Kafrawi, Ibrahim Mansour, Ghali Shukri, Radwa, and other writers whom I do not remember. Ghassan's murder was a quarter of a century ago now.

That day we were around fifty people. Yahya al-Taher 'Abdallah wrote out the placards in his beautiful calligraphy. We walked silently in the form of a funeral from Café Riche in Sulayman Pasha Street to the Journalists' Syndicate in 'Abd al-Khaliq Sarwat Street, and there the security forces were waiting for us. They took Yusuf Idris inside and we waited for him in the Syndicate's garden. The officer asked Yusuf Idris one specific question: "Did you have Palestinians with you in that march?"

Yusuf said: "I will give you the names of all fifty people. Write them down: Yusuf Idris, Yusuf Idris, Yusuf Idris, Yusuf Idris . . ."

Here the officer stopped him, ended the meeting, and left. Yusuf joined us in the garden, told us what had happened, and we split up.

Despite the sad occasion we could only laugh at one of the placards that Yahya had insisted on writing. It said: "They shoot horses, don't they?" When we went home and told Latifa al-Zayyat what we had done and about that particular placard, she unleashed her wide smile and said: "People must have had a good time laughing at you in the street. Why don't you write something they can understand?" When I told her what Yusuf Idris had done, she said: "That's Yusuf. He strikes a heroic posture, then stays confused and nervous and afraid, until he does its opposite. You were lucky."

What anniversary after today, Naji? And what birthday after today, Ghassan? What should we remember and what should we forget?

This is not a personal matter that concerns me alone. Our catastrophes and our pains are repeated and proliferate day after day. An event descends upon its opposite and destroys in us all anniversaries. Our calendars are broken, overlaid with pain, with bitter jokes and the smell of extinction. There are numbers now that can never again be neutral: they will always mean one thing. Since the defeat of June 1967 it is not possible for me to see the number '67' without it being tied to that defeat. I see it in part of a telephone number, on the door of a hotel room, on the license plate of a car, in any street in the world, on a cinema or theater ticket, on a page in a book, in the address of an office or a house, at the front of a train, or a flight number on an electronic board in any airport in the world. A number frozen in its frame. Not a number at all but a statue of a number, in wax, in granite, in lead, in indelible chalk on a blackboard in a black hall. It is not that I consider it a bad omen, just that I note it, that I register it. It moves from the unconscious to the conscious for a transient moment, then dives again like a dolphin that appears and disappears in the motions of the ocean. I do not draw any conclusions from this, do not tremble or become sad or tense. I just note it with all my five senses, as though it were a face that I know, a face that is part of my life and not part of it, but is always there, as we know that the dolphins are there in the water even though we do not see them. Is that June defeat a particular psychological problem for me? For my generation? For contemporary Arabs? Other events took place after it, other disappointments and setbacks no less dangerous. Wars raged, massacres were committed, political and intellectual discourses were altered, but '67' remains different. We are still paying its bills until this day. There is nothing that has happened in our contemporary history that does not bear a relationship to '67.

I was on my way back to my house in Mohandiseen in Cairo when I met by chance one of my closest friends of that period, Yahya al-Tahir 'Abdallah. The October 1973 war was in its fourth or fifth day, and he walked beside me in a state of noticeable happiness. Next to him I was gloomy and disturbed. He suddenly stopped in the middle of the street and said: "Why are you looking all miserable like a crow?"

"Yes, I'm a crow, because I can see things to caw over. This war, Yahya, will not end well."

On Tuesday, October 16, only ten days after the beginning of the war, I sat in front of the television in Latifa al-Zayyat's house listening with her to the speech of President Sadat in the Egyptian parliament. And there he was, wearing his military uniform furnished with decorations down to the belt and presenting what he called "my project for peace with Israel." The following day the talk of the Deversoir breach escalated noticeably. Days later, Henry Kissinger appeared in the area and events took their now well-known course, which ended with the visit of the president of the Arab Republic of Egypt to Israel and then to the Camp David Accords.

The Israeli flag was raised in Cairo just one hundred meters away from the statue of the 'Renaissance of Egypt,' in which the great sculptor Mahmoud Mukhtar immortalized the revolution of 1919. At University Bridge it flutters above the waters of the Nile only three hundred meters from the dome of Cairo University, the dome of all those sit-ins, the dome toward which once, long ago, when I was a young student at the university, I saw a procession of cars heading, out of which climbed Jawaharlal Nehru, Josip Broz Tito, Zhou Enlai, Kwame Nkrumah, and Gamal 'Abd al-Nasser. They climbed the marble staircase and sat in the Festival Hall, in front of them their papers and their files, and unforgettable words made their way from them into the consciousness of a young boy from the mountains of Deir Ghassanah. Words about independence, development, and freedom. Words, words, words, O Prince of Denmark!

I could not stand Sadat, his politics, the sound and sight of him, and under the dome of Cairo University in the winter of 1972, Radwa and I were with the students occupying the Nasser Hall. We would join their sit-in for part of the day or the whole day, and if the discussions and conversations carried us with them we would spend the night sleeping on the chairs. I did not realize the seriousness of this act of mine. The government considered every non-Egyptian in this kind of activity as an 'infiltrator.' A word I have always despised.

On the morning of January 24, I was surprised when Radwa came back home less than an hour after she had left. She had gone ahead of me to the university, carrying sandwiches she had prepared for the students. There were others who were doing the same thing. She said the University was surrounded by security forces and they were preventing anyone going on to the campus. Later, we found out that the police had arrested all the students involved in the sit-in and driven them to jail. The girls and boys looked out from the windows of the police vans with eyes red from the continual late nights and the exhaustion of sleeping in chairs. They looked at the streets of Cairo sleeping in that sad, defeated dawn, and threw out of the windows scraps of paper on which they had written three words: "Wake up Egypt."

Since 1967 the last move in the Arab chess game has been a losing move. A move backward, negating everything that came before it, however positive those opening moves were. After the Battle of al-Karama, which the Palestinians and the Jordanians fought together against the enemy, we turned in Black September against ourselves. After the war of 1973 and the crossing of the Suez Canal we went to Camp David. After our opposition to Camp David we Arabized it and generalized it and accepted what was even less useful and more scandalous. After the Israeli invasion of Lebanon the PLO turned from heroic resistance to fighting within itself and moderation and adaptability in face of the conditions set by the enemy. After the popular Intifada on the land of Palestine we went to Oslo. We are always adapting to the conditions of the enemy. Since '67 we have been adapting. And here is Benyamin Netanyahu, prime minister of Israel, calming America's fears for the current agreement by saying that the Arabs will in the end adapt to his harshness because they always adapt to whatever they have to.

Do I have a problem with '67? Yes, I have a problem. The defeat of June is not over. On the second day of the war, and with the national songs and anthems growing louder and louder on the radio, university students poured into the centers set up to process volunteers for the front. I stood in the line of volunteers and registered my name. They gave me a small green card with my name written on it and underneath it one sentence: "To be called to serve on June 12, 1967."

And on June 9, I sat in front of the television in my flat in

Zamalek, watching Gamal 'Abd al-Nasser speak as the whole nation hung on his lips that night, trying to understand something of what had happened, was still happening, at the front. The owner of the flat, a blonde and extremely large woman whom I called Madame Sosostris, sat next to me, and we heard him say: "We have suffered a setback." Then he declared that he would step down completely and finally, relinquishing all his official posts. I jumped out of my seat, to the door, to the street, and found myself one of millions of people who jumped at that same moment into the darkness of the streets and the darkness of the future.

There was not a gap of minutes or even seconds between the ear and the step. I saw an entire society spreading out in the streets in the blink of an eye. We spent the night in the streets and on the bridges over the river, moving with no apparent objective. We lived in the streets until the evening of the following day. And when the days and the years had passed, we knew that we had been taking part in what historians later called the demonstrations of June 9 and 10, which put 'Abd al-Nasser back in the seat of power.

Nobody after that called us up for the voluntary service. The Six Day War ended with Nasser's speech. The future of the people remained mysterious and every time they announced that they would clarify it, it became more mysterious. The mystery grew with the death of Nasser, and then again with Sadat taking over the presidency. It grew with the October War and with the Camp David Agreement that stated clearly that the October War was the last and final war. Our future grew more mysterious, more unknown with the Israeli invasion of Lebanon, then the War of the Camps, then Oslo. And it is still mysterious, now, today.

Since June 5, 1967 we have been left to sort out our lives in the lengthening shadow of the defeat, the defeat that has not yet ended.

That is the one definite milestone for what followed and is following until now. Yes, '67 has been stamped permanently on my mind since I lived it in my early youth.

I know I would be no good at professional political work because I react to the world with feelings and with intuition. This does not go well with the necessities of politics. I cannot, if I march in a demonstration, shout slogans. I may join a demonstration to advertise my position but I cannot raise my voice to cry out slogans or demands, however convinced of them I may be. The images of demonstrations that remain in my mind are rather comic ones of men carried high on shoulders, chanting rhythmic slogans, and as happens in Eisenstein's films, these earnest chanters transform into giant open mouths full of irregular white teeth, crowding the entire scene in the memory. As for the waving of arms and the raised fists, hitting the air above the demonstration, there have been times when they have made me laugh despite my embarrassment and my fear that my laughter would be taken amiss by those around me.

Abu Tawfiq used to get into the jeep belonging to the media services and drive around the streets of Fakihani in Beirut repeating the unchanging phrase "O our beautiful martyr!" He would then start to recount the virtues of the martyr we had just lost. At first the scene was moving. But the repetition of the falling of martyrs, the repetition of the funerals, the repetition of his favorite sentence, "O our beautiful martyr!" started to color the tragedy with a tint of routine familiarity, and into our day's sadness it would bring a strange kind of comedy.

The comedy of death, of funerals. Long struggles that take up tens of years of people's lives leave shadows of courage and fortitude, but also leave shadows of nihilism and a mockery of the available destinies. These shadows are darkened by the repeated retreats that follow each attempt to move forward. Mockery becomes one of the psychological tools that enable us to continue.

Abu Tawfiq became accustomed to loss as the martyrs became accustomed to the repetition of their sacrifice, and as we who walked in their funerals became accustomed to seeing them off with the same slogans and noise to their metaphorical destination—Palestine—and their actual destination—the grave. The walls of Fakihani were covered with posters that bore their faces, but as more and more martyrs fell, the posters crowded each other on the walls, the newer faces covering parts of the older ones. Funerals were an integral part of the lives of Palestinians wherever they were, in the homeland or in exile, in the days of their calm and the days of their Intifada, in the days of their wars and the days of their peace punctuated by massacres.

So, when Yitzhak Rabin spoke so eloquently of the tragedy of Israelis as absolute victims, and the eyes of his listeners in the White House garden and in the whole world grew wet, I knew that I would not forget for a long time his words that day:

"We are the victims of war and violence. We have not known a year or a month when mothers have not mourned their sons."

I felt that tremor that I know so well and which I feel when I know that I have not done my best, that I have failed: Rabin has taken everything, even the story of our death.

This leader knew how to demand that the world should respect Israeli blood, the blood of every Israeli individual without exception. He knew how to demand that the world should respect Israeli tears, and he was able to present Israel as the victim of a crime perpetrated by us. He changed facts, he altered the order of things, he presented us as the initiators of violence in the Middle East and said what he said with eloquence, with clarity and conviction. I remember every word Rabin said that day:

"We, the soldiers coming back from the war, smeared with blood, we saw our brothers and our friends killed in front of us, we attended their funerals unable to look into the eyes of their mothers. Today we remember each one of them with eternal love."

It is easy to blur the truth with a simple linguistic trick: start your story from "Secondly." Yes, this is what Rabin did. He simply neglected to speak of what happened first. Start your story with "Secondly," and the world will be turned upside-down. Start your story with "Secondly," and the arrows of the Red Indians are the original criminals and the guns of the white men are entirely the victim. It is enough to start with "Secondly," for the anger of the black man against the white to be barbarous. Start with "Secondly," and Gandhi becomes responsible for the tragedies of the British. You only need to start your story with "Secondly," and the burned Vietnamese will have wounded the humanity of the napalm, and Victor Jara's songs will be the shameful thing and not Pinochet's bullets, which killed so many thousands in the Santiago stadium. It is enough to start the story with "Secondly," for my grandmother, Umm 'Ata, to become the criminal and Ariel Sharon her victim.

What can Abu Tawfiq's jeep do in the middle of all this absurdity? The Israelis occupy our homes as victims and present us to the world as killers. Israel dazzles the world with its generosity toward us. Rabin said:

"Signing the Declaration of Principles is not easy for me as a fighter in the Israeli Army and in its wars. It is not easy for the people of Israel or for the Jews of the Diaspora."

The houses built on top of ours gallantly declare their willingness to understand our odd predilection toward living in camps scattered in the Diaspora of gods and flies, as though we had begged them to throw us out of our homes and to send their bulldozers to destroy them in front of our very eyes. Their generous guns in Deir Yassin forgive us the fact that they piled our bodies high at the sunset hour there one day. Their fighter jets forgive the graves of our martyrs in Beirut. Their soldiers forgive the tendency of our teenagers' bones to break. Israel the victim polishes its hot, red knife with the sheen of forgiveness.

In the global celebration no one—not even we, the people who speak for him—remembered Abu Tawfiq's beautiful martyr.

9

THE DAILY DAY
OF JUDGMENT

The pillow is the register of our lives. The first draft of our story that, each new night, we write without ink and tell without a sound. It is the field of memory that has been plowed and fertilized and watered in the darkness that is ours.

Each person has his darkness.

Each person has his right to darkness.

These are the scribbles that come to the mind without order, without structure. The pillow is our white cotton court of law, smooth to the touch, cruel of sentence. When it has received our heads, crowded with joy and contentment or loss and shame, the pillow becomes a conscience. The pillow is our daily Day of Judgment. A personal Day of Judgment for each one of us who remains alive. An early Day of Judgment that does not wait for our final entry to eternal peace.

Our small sins for which no law takes us to task and that are known only to careful suppression spread out in the darkness of night in the light of pillows that know, pillows that do not keep secrets and do not care to defend the sleeper.

Our beauty, invisible to eyes spoiled by familiarity and haste, our worthiness, cruelly violated each day, are retrieved only here, and it is only because we retrieve them here every night that we are able to continue with the game. With life.

The pillow claims nothing. A microphone may lie. Tender words of love, pulpits, figures, letters, reports, preachers, leaders, doctors, a mother—may lie. The pillow is woven out of truth. Truth as a secret, hidden by the calculations of daytime.

The defeated may claim victory and believe himself. When he puts his head down on his small pillow it tells him the truth, even if he should deny it. I did not win. He says it to himself without opening his mouth. And if he does not dare, the pillow will dare: you did not win. He may appear once again as a victor in public. He may be supported by some. But those some too will feel that cold tremor when alone in the night of their calculated positions and their patched-together support.

The worth of life, the assertion of self, a feeling of pride, an adoption of one story rather than another—all these certainties assured by day, in the dust of the crowd, in the fever of competition and conflict, are turned by our pillows into hypotheses. The pillow is the misgivings that demand to be examined mercilessly.

Lying on my back in bed, my locked fingers cradling my head, I do not know what keeps my eyes open gazing toward the ceiling. The ceiling is no longer there in this complete darkness, but sleep has nothing to do with me. It was invented for others. This is my final night in Ramallah. My final night in this small room, under a window that looks out on countless questions, looks out also on a settlement. As though by crossing that small wooden bridge I managed to stand in front of my days. I made my days stand in front of me. I touched particular details for no reason and neglected others, also for no reason. I chattered an entire lifetime to myself while my guests thought I was silent.

I crossed the forbidden bridge and suddenly I bent to collect my scattered fragments as I would collect the flaps of my coat together on an icy day, or as a pupil would collect his papers scattered by the wind of the fields as he comes back from far away. On the pillow I collected the days and nights of laughter, of anger, of tears, of foolishness, and of marble monuments for which a single lifetime cannot suffice to visit them all with an offering of silence and respect.

I prepare my small bag, ready to return to the bridge, to Amman, then Cairo, and then to Morocco to read poetry at a festival in Rabat. I will spend less than a week in Rabat, then return to Cairo, and then with Radwa and Tamim to spend the summer with my mother and 'Alaa in Amman. In Amman I will wait for Tamim's permit. I will return here with him. He will see it. He will see me in it, and we shall ask all the questions after that.

Tonight, with everyone in the house asleep and morning about to break, I ask a question that the days have never answered:

What deprives the spirit of its colors?
What is it other than the bullets of the invaders that have hit the
   body?

GLOSSARY

'Ammu/'Amm: paternal uncle or great-uncle, or, more generally, a respectful form of address to any man of an older generation. **'Ammi:** my *'amm*.

Abu Hayyan al-Tawhidi: eleventh-century philosopher and mystic writer.

al-Manfaluti: Arab writer, 1876–1924, famous for his oversentimental style.

Badr Shakir al-Sayyab: Iraqi poet, 1926–64, the first to challenge the classical form of Arabic poetry.

Bismillah: 'In the name of God'—Sadat began all his speeches thus, stretching out the final vowel.

dabka: traditional Palestinian dance performed by young men in a row or circle, arms around shoulders.

Fayruz: the greatest living Arab woman singer.

Giddu: grandfather.

Ghassan Kanafani: much-respected Palestinian writer who was assassinated by an Israeli car bomb in 1972.

Hajja: a woman who has performed the pilgrimage to Mecca; or, more generally, a respectful form of address to an older woman.

'Id: either one of two major festivals in the Islamic calendar, *'Id al-Fitr* at the end of the fasting month of Ramadan, or *'Id al-Adha* two months later.

Khal: maternal uncle or great-uncle. **Khali:** my *khal*.

Khala: maternal aunt or great-aunt, or, more generally, a respectful form of address to any woman of an older generation. **Khalti:** my *khala*.

khawaja: a form of address to a non-Arab.

Kitab al-aghani: a comprehensive literary history compiled by al-Asfahani in the tenth century.

kufiya: the traditional headdress of the men of some Arab countries, including Palestine.

kunafa: a sweet pastry of fine noodles, often stuffed with white cheese and covered in syrup.

Latifa al-Zayyat: prominent Egyptian novelist, activist, and university professor, 1923–96.

Mahmoud Darwish: prominent Palestinian poet.

Naji al-'Ali: the best-known Palestinian cartoonist, assassinated in London in 1987.

qatayef: small, sweet pancakes, rolled and filled with nuts or cream.

Sitti: my grandmother

THE QUESTION OF PALESTINE
by Edward W. Said

When it was first published in this country in 1977, this original and
provocative book made Palestine the subject of a serious debate—
one that is now more critical than ever. A Palestinian by birth and
once a member of the Palestinian National Council, Said brings to
the question of Palestine an exile's passion, as well as the rigorous
scholarship that distinguished his influential *Orientalism*. In this
compelling book, Said traces the fatal collision between two peoples
in the Middle East and its repercussions in the lives of both the occupier and the occupied—as well as in the conscience of the West.

Vintage Books • Current Affairs/Middle Eastern History • 0-679-73988-2

THE END OF THE PEACE PROCESS
by Edward W. Said

In this powerful collection of essays, written mostly for Arab and
European newspapers and previously not readily available to
American readers, Said uncovers the political mechanism that adver-
tises reconciliation in the Middle East while keeping peace out of the
picture. Said cites the imbalance of power that prohibits real negotiations and promotes the second-class treatment of Palestinians. In
this unflinching cry for civic justice and self-determination, Said promotes not a political agenda but a transcendent alternative: the
peaceful coexistence of Arabs and Jews enjoying shared citizenship.

Vintage Books • Current Affairs/Middle Eastern Studies • 0-375-72574-1

ECHOES OF AN AUTOBIOGRAPHY
by Naguib Mahfouz

Echoes of an Autobiography provides a unique opportunity to catch
an intimate glimpse into the life and mind of magnificent storyteller
and Nobel Prize winner Naguib Mahfouz. Here, in his first work of
nonfiction ever to be published in the United States, Mahfouz considers the myriad perplexities of existence, including preoccupations
with old age, death, and life's transitory nature. A surprising and
delightful departure from his much-loved fiction, this unusual and
thoughtful book proves that Mahfouz is not only a "storyteller of the
first order" (*Vanity Fair*), but also a profound thinker.

Anchor Books • Autobiography • 0-385-48556-5

IN THE EYE OF THE SUN
by Ahdaf Soueif

Set amidst the turmoil of contemporary Middle Eastern politics, this vivid novel offers a window into the often hidden lives of Arab women today. It tells the story of Asya, a brilliant young woman who grows up in the luxurious world of the Egyptian elite, marries a Westernized husband, and pursues graduate study in England, where she becomes embroiled in a love affair with an Englishman. But for all her worldliness, Asya remains caught in a struggle between her ties to tradition and her desire for independence and sexual fulfillment. Lyrical and honest, sensual and erudite, *In the Eye of the Sun* is a revealing account of cultural collision.

Anchor Books • Fiction/Middle Eastern Studies • 0-385-72037-8

THE MAP OF LOVE
by Ahdaf Soueif

Isabel Parkman, an American journalist, has fallen in love with a gifted and difficult Egyptian-American conductor. Shadowing her romance is the courtship of her great-grandparents Anna and Sharif. In 1900, the recently widowed Anna Winterbourne left England for Egypt, an outpost of the Empire roiling with political sentiment. She soon found herself enraptured by the real Egypt and in love with Sharif Pasha al-Baroudi, an Egyptian nationalist. When Isabel, in an attempt to discover the truth behind her heritage, reenacts Anna's excursion to Egypt, the story of her great-grandparents unravels before her, revealing startling parallels to her own life.

Anchor Books • Fiction/Literature • 0-385-72011-4

SEVEN PILLARS OF WISDOM
by T. E. Lawrence

In this monumental epic, Lawrence tells the story of his role in the Arab revolt against the Turks, a minor diversionary theater of war for the British immersed in World War I, but a profoundly meaningful struggle for the Arabs. What has lent the books its lasting fascination is Lawrence's passionate account of the Arab people and of an Arab nation struggling to be born. The parallels to be drawn with the ongoing conflict in the Middle East are undeniable. Not only a consummate military history, but also a colorful saga and a lyrical exploration of the mind of a great man, *Seven Pillars of Wisdom* has become an indisputable classic.

Anchor Books • Middle Eastern Studies/Literature • 0-385-41895-7

THE DREAM PALACE OF THE ARABS
by Fouad Ajami

From Fouad Ajami, the acclaimed chronicler of Arab politics, comes this absorbing account of how a generation of Arab intellectuals tried to introduce cultural renewals in their homelands through the forces of modernity and secularism. Ultimately, they came to face disappointment, exile, and, on occasion, death. Brilliantly weaving together the strands of a tumultuous century in Arab political thought, history, and poetry, Ajami's remarkable book is both a clear-eyed analysis of public matters—the history of a people and its ideas—and a personal inquiry into the author's own experience.

Vintage Books • Current Affairs/Middle Eastern History • 0-375-70474-4

THE ARAB WORLD
by Elizabeth Warnock Fernea and Robert Fernea

Vast political and economic shifts have transformed the Middle East since the 1985 edition of this award-winning work. The Ferneas, leading scholars in Middle Eastern studies, felt the need to return to the towns and cities they had written about to see how these changes had affected the region and the people who live in it. With new chapters on Baghdad, Beirut, Amman, Jerusalem, Marrakesh, and Cairo, this updated and expanded edition of *The Arab World* takes readers beyond the corridors of power to the most candid of kitchen-table confidences, revealing the human face of the Arab world.

Anchor Books • Middle Eastern Studies/Current Affairs • 0-385-48520-4

VINTAGE BOOKS • ANCHOR BOOKS
Available at your local bookstore, or call toll-free to order:
1-800-793-2665 (credit cards only).